Seafood
Pasta &
Noodles

THE NEW CLASSICS

Rosina Tinari Wilson

Illustrated by Marlene McLoughlin

Ten Speed Press

TEN SPEED PRESS
P.O. Box 7123
Berkeley, California 94707

Cover and text design by Fifth Street Design, Berkeley, CA

Library of Congress Cataloging-in-Publication Data

Wilson, Rosina Tinari.
    Seafood, pasta & noodles : the new classics / by Rosina Tinari
  Wilson ; illustrated by Marlene McLoughlin.
        p. cm.
    Includes index.
    ISBN 0-89815-603-3 (paper) ISBN 0-89815-668-8 (hardcover)
    1. Cookery (Seafood) 2. Cookery (Pasta) I. Title.   II. Title:
Seafood, pasta, and noodles.
  TX747. W556 1994
  641.6 ' 92 — dc20   93-49012
            CIP

FIRST PRINTING 1994

Printed in Korea

2 3 4 5 — 98 97 96 95

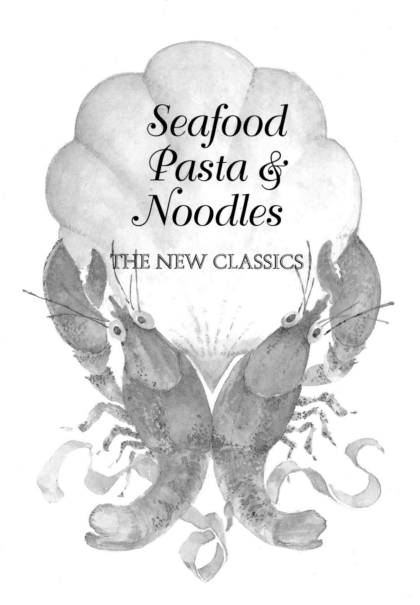

Seafood Pasta & Noodles

THE NEW CLASSICS

For my mother,
Marie Chericone Tinari —
My first cooking teacher
and the best there is

Acknowledgements

Heartfelt thanks to my eternally eager guinea pigs: my loving hubby Wayne, daughter Siri, and parents Marie (a *terrific* cook and teacher!) and Lou; to Barbara, Bob and Merry, Catherine, Diana, Feliziz, Jodi, Judy and Peter, and Judy for their on-target suggestions and hands-on help; to Irene, my skillful, cheerful and absolutely tireless testing partner, who helped transform each recipe from a rough prototype into a carefully measured and timed reality; to Cubby and the gang at Tokyo Fish Market for all the special orders, last-minute requests and downright perfect seafood; to Jackie, Christine and Alexis, my meticulous and good-natured editors at Ten Speed Press; and to Marlene, whose exquisite watercolors bring *Seafood Pasta and Noodles – The New Classics* to life.

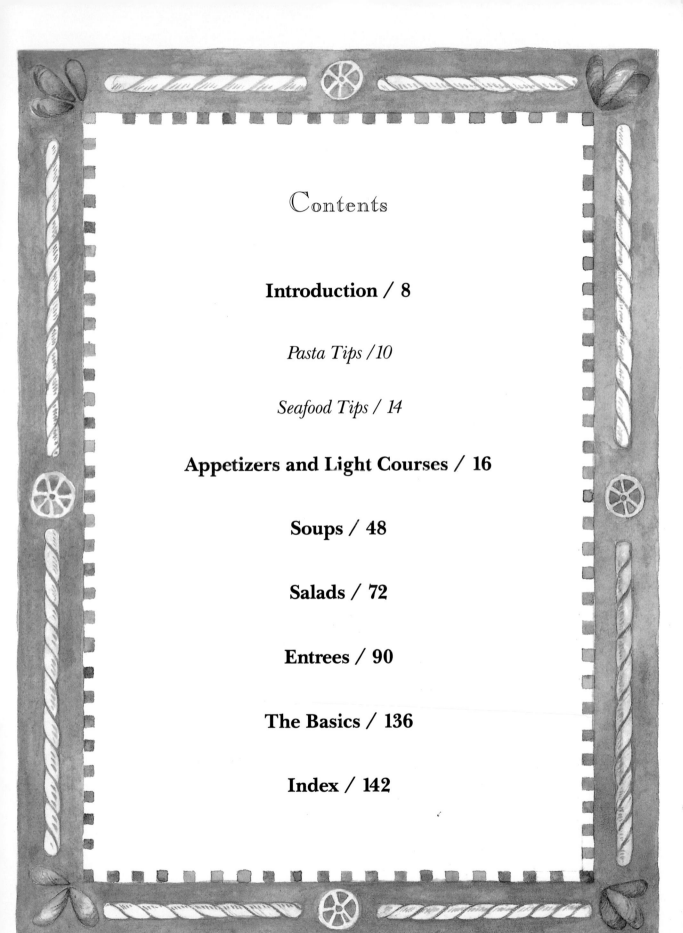

Contents

INTRODUCTION

Seafood Pasta and Noodles — The New Classics is a celebration of two of our most popular and versatile, fast and healthful foods. Its one-hundred-plus recipes, some traditional, others deliciously contemporary, combine pasta and noodles in myriad shapes with a piscine pot-pourri from the waters of the world. You'll find soups, stews and chowders; salads; appetizers and light courses; and, of course, entrees — something for every occasion, whether it's a quiet supper at home or a festive buffet for a crowd.

In many of these recipes, the seafood and pasta share equal billing: Tagliarine with Scallops and Hazel-Basil Pesto, for instance, or Halibut with Ziti and Olive-Rosemary Tapenade. In others, such as Pan-Seared Trout in Black Bean Sauce or Linguine with Cioppino, the seafood is the star, with the noodles playing a supporting role. Others, such as Saracen Spaghettini, put pasta in the spotlight. Some show off pasta and noodles — whether it's cannelloni from the West or potstickers from the East — as the perfect container for a seafood stuffing. And some recipes turn that idea inside out, using the pasta as a filling for shellfish or garden-fresh vegetables.

You will discover culinary treasures passed down to us from the tables of Old Europe and stockpots of Asia, revitalized with seafood and pasta. (Many are low in added fat and cholesterol, although die-hard dairy lovers will be relieved to hear that they can revel in the likes of Fettuccine Alfredo with Lobster!) And you'll find many brand new creations which fuse the best ingredients and techniques from all over the world in freewheeling style. Twirl your pasta fork and dissolve national boundaries into one grand gastronomic cooking pot!

Each recipe offers a drinks suggestion, to give you the most enjoyment possible. Whether it's a crisp white wine or a fruity red, a frosty mug of beer or a refreshing pitcher of iced tea, a well-chosen beverage will not only enhance the flavor of your meal but will, in turn, be enhanced by it. So, let's raise a glass in hearty toast. *Salute* — to your health!

> Unless otherwise stated, all recipes serve four to six.
> * alongside a recipe means it is quick to prepare.

Pasta Tips

Canny cooks the world over already know that pasta doesn't just make for delicious meals, but also healthful and wholesome ones. Loaded with complex carbohydrates, it's virtually free of fat, salt and cholesterol. It's also a boon to the budget-conscious. Dressed down, pasta satisfies a growing family with hearty appetites. Gussied up, it stretches expensive ingredients to impress the guests at your next dinner party.

The recipes here use commercial dry pasta unless otherwise specified. Where fresh pasta is called for, buy it from a specialty shop or your local supermarket's refrigerator case. Better yet, make your own from the recipes in the Basics section (pages 136–141).

Cooking Pasta

When cooking Italian-style pasta, made with wheat flour, use *lots* of boiling water — at least 4 quarts per pound (2 L per 500 g), and I prefer twice that amount. (The more water you have, the less time it takes to start boiling again after you add the pasta.) Put the kettle on at least 20 minutes before you plan to cook the noodles so you'll be ready to go. Add the pasta all at once, so it will cook evenly. Stir it well to avoid clumping. Cover the pot until the water returns to the boil. Uncover and stir again.

Start timing your pasta from when the water returns to the boil. Cooking times will depend on the pasta shape, of course, on whether it's fresh or dry, and even from brand to brand. The recipes give rough cooking times where appropriate, but the best way to tell if it's done is to taste it frequently until it is just cooked through. Dry pasta should be slightly firm, with a bit of bite to it (*al dente*, as the Italians say, "to the tooth"). Fresh should be a bit more tender, resisting your teeth only slightly.

If you're cooking nest-shaped noodles, you'll need to simmer them very carefully to keep the nests intact. A two-part kettle with a steamer insert is helpful. (Scoop nests out gently with a large slotted spoon instead of draining.)

Although some Asian-style noodles should also be boiled, those made with rice, cornstarch (powder) or mung beans are simply soaked in hot water until tender. The thicker the noodle, the hotter the water and the longer the soak.

Drain your noodles immediately — less thoroughly if you want a soupier consistency, as you might in Linguine with Clam Sauce, say. Many people rinse the pasta at this point, but I only do if I'm preparing a salad or cold dish, to cool the pasta down quickly. Instead, I prefer to combine the noodles immediately with the rest of the prepared ingredients.

If you have leftovers, replace the moisture that has been absorbed by the noodles with more sauce, if you have it, or a touch of water, stock, olive oil or butter. Since pasta soaks up flavor, it often tastes even better the next night!

Pasta Glossary

There are literally hundreds of different shapes and sizes of pasta the world over. For each type there is often, traditionally, a very specific use; others bring an unexpectedly original touch to a dish. In case you can't always find the one called for in a recipe, here are a few simple guidelines.

Try to match the actual size of the pasta (after cooking) with that of the other ingredients in the recipe — the results are pleasing to both eye and palate. Consider the overall tone of the dish: for a clear, delicate broth, choose tiny shapes, such as acini di pepe, or fragile Asian-style noodles. For a hearty stew, boil up large elbows, say, or robust egg noodles. Light, simple sauces would get lost on lasagne, but they're perfect on vermicelli. And chunky toppings that would overpower dainty angelhair come into their own on husky rigatoni. Hollow pastas, such as bucatini, and textured ones, such as penne, take on extra flavor because they have so many surfaces to absorb and trap sauces and seasonings. They're also less likely to skid off your fork!

A short language lesson might help you in selecting the more popular Italian-style pastas because they come in so many different sizes and forms. Names ending in *-elle* or *-elli, -ette* or *-etti, -ine* or *-ini* mean smaller sizes: *spaghettini* is thinner than *spaghetti,* for instance. An *-one* or *-oni* ending, or the word *grande,* means it's large. *Rigate/i* means the surface is ridged (*lisce/i* means it isn't). *Ricci* or *riccie* refers to a ruffled edge.

Italian-Style

acini di pepe — "peppercorns"; tiny pellets for soup

agnolotti — round or semicircular, stuffed, often with ruffled edges

anelli — "rings"; for soups or delicate sauces

angelhair — also called capelli d'angelo; often sold twisted into nests

bucatini — long, thin, hollow rods

cannelloni — "large reeds"; big tubes for stuffing (when using sheets of fresh pasta, roll them around the filling)

capelli d'angelo — see angelhair

capellini — "fine hairs"; very thin spaghetti

cavatappi — "corkscrews"; short, hollow spirals

conchiglie — "conch shells"; the small sizes are good for soups and light sauces, the largest can be stuffed

creste di gallo — "cockscombs"; medium-sized with ridges and ruffles

ditalini — "little thimbles"; short tubes, good in soups

elbows — semicircular tubes longer than ditalini

farfalle — "butterflies"; also called bowties, medium-sized and textured

fettuccine — flat, ribbon-shaped noodles, about $\frac{1}{8}$ to $\frac{1}{4}$ inch/.3 to .5 cm wide

filini — "little threads"; short pieces of vermicelli

fusilli — corkscrew-shaped, either short *(corti),* like penne, or long *(lunghi),* like spaghetti

gemelli — "twins"; two short strands of spaghetti twisted together

gnocchi — small dumplings made of flour or potatoes

lasagne — broad, flat noodles, with or without ruffled edges, usually layered with filling and baked

linguine — "little tongues"; like spaghetti, but flat

lumache — "snails"; short, wide tubes, folded in at one end

maccheroni — macaroni; long hollow rods

mafalde — wide noodles with ruffled edges, similar to pappardelle

manicotti — "muffs"; to be stuffed like cannelloni; made with either pasta dough or light pancakes

margherita — "daisy"; like mafalde, but ruffled on one side only

maruzzelle — shell-shaped, similar to conchiglie

mostaccioli — "little mustaches"; medium-sized tubes cut diagonally; similar to penne and available in either smooth or ridged

occhi di lupo — "wolf's eyes"; like large ziti

orecchiette — "little ears"; tiny indented discs

orzo — "barley"; little pellets good in soup or as a substitute for rice; also called riso or rosa marina

pappardelle — broad noodles, $\frac{1}{2}$ to 1 inch/1.5 to 2.5 cm wide; use a fluted pastry wheel when cutting homemade pappardelle to create ruffled edges

pastina — tiny, star-shaped pasta for soups and stuffings

penne — "quill pens"; like mostaccioli and available either smooth or ridged

perciatelli — long, hollow rods, similar to bucatini

ravioli — stuffed fresh pasta squares, usually with fluted edges

riccini — small, twisted pasta with a curled edge

rigatoni — "large ridged" pasta; similar to mostaccioli rigati, but cut straight across

riso — "rice"; like orzo, it can substitute for rice

rotelle — "cartwheels"; also called rotini, ruote di carro or, simply, wagon wheels, which they resemble; confusingly, the names rotelle and rotini are also used for short fusilli

seme di melone — "melon seeds"; similar to orzo

spaghetti — "little strings"; long, thin, solid rods

spaghettini — long solid rods, thinner than spaghetti

stelle — "stars"; for soups, stuffings, or as a rice substitute

tagliatelle — flat noodles, about $\frac{1}{4}$ inch/.5 cm wide; also called tagliarine

tortelli — small stuffed fresh pasta; tortellini are smaller still, tortelloni larger

trenette — flat noodles, similar to fettuccine

tubetti — "little tubes"; small, hollow and similar to ditalini

vermicelli — "little worms"; long rods like spaghetti, but much thinner

ziti — "bridegrooms"; medium-sized tubes, like large penne, but cut straight across

Asian-Style

bean threads — China and Southeast Asia; also called glass or cellophane noodles or saifun; made from mung-bean starch

cornstarch sticks — called bihon in the Philippines; similar to glass noodles in appearance and preparation

gyoza — Japanese potstickers

mein — fresh or dried Chinese noodles made of wheat flour; available in several widths

pansit (pancit) — Philippine wheat noodles; often stir-fried; Pancit Canton (similar to Cantonese chow mein noodles) come precooked

potstickers — Chinese filled dumplings; semicircular shape fried on one side; wrapper resembles round shao-mai wrapper

rice paper — Southeast Asian (especially Vietnamese); thin, stiff circles about 8 inches/20 cm diameter; often used for spring rolls

rice sticks — Chinese and Southeast Asian; also called maifun, banh pho; available in several widths

shao-mai — Chinese; similar to wonton wrappers, but round; also called siu mai

shirataki — Japanese yam thread noodles; available fresh and water-packed; often used in sukiyaki

soba — Japanese dried noodles; often made with buckwheat flour, sometimes flavored with green tea (cha soba); served cold or in broth

somen — Japanese wheat noodles; available in several colors; often served cold

udon — Japanese wheat noodles; available fresh or dried; often served in broth

wonton wrappers — Chinese; made of wheat; usually in squares about 3 inches/7.5 cm (but sometimes round); available fresh in several thicknesses; stuffed and served fried with sauces or poached in soups

Seafood Tips

Like pasta, seafood is a tremendous boon to busy home cooks. Generally low in fat and calories, it's also quick, nutritious and versatile. Whether it sports shells or fins, whether it hails from ocean, bay, river or lake, it too has universal appeal.

Selecting Seafood

The three keys to buying seafood are freshness, freshness and freshness. Fish and shellfish have delicate flesh that spoils quickly, so unless you're lucky enough to catch it yourself, find a reputable store you can trust. Small independent fish markets that replenish their stock daily are ideal; but a well-staffed fish counter at your local supermarket can fill the bill nicely, if it has rapid turnover.

Whole fish, also known as fish "in the round," will have glistening skin, clear eyes that seem to stare right back at you and a neutral, saltwaterlike odor. Steaks (crosscut slices on the bone) or fillets (lengthwise sections sliced off the back-bone) should look moist, translucent and somewhat shiny. There should be no breaks in the flesh: it should be firm and spring back to the touch.

Many types of shellfish, (unless of course, precooked) should still be alive when you buy them. Lobsters should be waving their claws and snapping their tails; crabs, trying to scuttle off the table. Bivalves such as mussels, clams and oysters should have unbroken, tightly closed shells. If there's a slight gap, give it a tap, and accept only those that close up immediately. Shrimp and prawns usually come in frozen, then are thawed at the market. They should look glossy, with moist, translucent meat, and have a clean briny smell. Scallops, whether the small, sweet bay scallops or larger sea scallops, should be creamy rather than white in color. Again, sniff for that smell of the sea.

It's always better to buy fresh rather than frozen fish. If my seafood suggestion in your chosen recipe doesn't look its best at market that day, substitute something similar that *is* in its prime. If you have no choice, defrost your fish slowly in the fridge. And don't store frozen fish too long — home freezers are not cold enough to prevent deterioration and flavor loss. Many fish, especially those with delicate flesh, lose texture when frozen raw. If you have a surplus, you're better off freezing some *after* cooking.

Preparing Seafood

Live lobsters and crabs should be plunged into a large kettle of boiling water and cooked, covered, until their shells turn bright red. When cool enough to handle, crack the claws — and, with lobster, the tail — with a nutcracker to extract the tender meats. Save lobster and crab shells in your freezer to add to your next seafood stock.

Mussels and clams can be somewhat sandy, both inside and out. Soak them in salted cold water for up to an hour, then scrub them well. Try to slide the shells apart as you wash each one. Discard any that separate. For mussels, pull off any "beards" (the stiff threads at the base that tether them to their home rocks). Unless a recipe specifies otherwise, you can serve mussels and clams in their shells: the colors and textures are very appealing.

To clean *prawns and shrimp,* twist off the heads, if any. Hold the tail away from you and the curved back upwards. With a pair of scissors, cut along the back from head end to tail through both the shell and about ¼ inch/.5 cm of the flesh. Unless the recipe says to leave the shell on, peel it away and tug gently on the tail to remove it. Remove and discard the dark vein running down the back. Again, save the shells in the freezer to enrich your next fish stock.

Squid, or calamari, is inexpensive, delectable and not nearly as intimidating to clean as you might imagine. Cut off the cluster of tentacles just above the eyes and set them aside to include, whole, halved or chopped, in your recipe. Squeeze out the small, round "beak," then gently pull out the long, flexible "quill" (it looks like a strip of clear plastic) from the body of the squid. Then squeeze out the white material inside the body and discard it along with the beak and quill. If you wish, peel away the skin. Your tubes of squid are now ready to slice into rings or to stuff.

APPETIZERS
AND
LIGHT COURSES

There's nothing more appetizing than an appetizer — a tasty nibble that triggers your taste buds for a full-course feast. It tempts the most finicky eater; it turns the plainest meal into a party. Pop a savory morsel into your mouth and you'll stave off hunger pangs while you gear up for the treats to come.

Seafood and pasta team perfectly to prime your palate for a festive dinner. Choose a make-ahead recipe, such as tangy Mediterranean Stuffed Peppers or Greek-accented Riso and Shrimp Grape Leaves, and let the tantalizing fragrance fill your kitchen even before the doorbell rings. Or opt for hands-on entertaining and let everyone roll their own Sushi-Seasoned Glass Noodle Rolls.

You can mix and match these appetizers, as I often do, or create a theme that ties them together. Try, for instance, a colorful Pacific Rim array of California Rice Paper Rolls, East-West Tuna Tartare, Seafood Potstickers with Minted Mango Salsa and Lobster-Macadamia Wonton Ravioli. Pass them around with assorted cocktails when guests first arrive, or turn them into a delicious *dim sum*-style buffet.

For, as you'll discover, the "Appetizers and Light Courses" that follow are amazingly versatile. They serve not only as tempting lead-ins to a leisurely dinner, but also as creative options for flexible menu planning. Many are even filling enough to do double duty as light entrees.

Looking for a lavish showstopper for Sunday brunch? An upscale, quick-to-fix nosh after a night on the town? Try the luxurious Vermicelli with Caviar or creamy Fettuccine with Smoked Salmon. When you're home alone, treat yourself to a snack of Green-Tea Soba with Tamari-Ginger Sauce. Or tote a crowd-pleasing Picnic Frittata to the beach or ballpark.

So relax, sit back and raise a glass with family and friends. Then bring on the appetizers and watch them disappear — and let the compliments begin!

Stuffed Mussels with Sun-Dried Tomatoes

This flavorful finger-food appetizer gives you lots of flexibility for party planning. You can make the stuffing a day in advance, if you like, then steam and stuff the mussels several hours before your guests arrive.

3 oz/90 g filini, or 1-inch/2.5 cm pieces of vermicelli, cooked (see page 10)

∙

5 dozen mussels (about 3½ lb/1.75 kg)
1 cup/250 mL/8 fl oz white wine

Stuffing
2 medium onions, finely chopped
¼ cup/60 mL/2 fl oz olive oil
4 cloves garlic, finely minced
½ cup/30 g/1 oz unseasoned bread crumbs
½ cup/90 g/3 oz oil-packed sun-dried tomatoes, drained and finely chopped
2 tablespoons lemon juice
1 tablespoon fresh oregano or marjoram leaves, finely minced
¼ to ½ teaspoon cayenne (optional)
Salt and freshly ground pepper to taste

∙

Lemon wedges
Oregano or marjoram sprigs

Steam mussels with wine until they open, about 5 minutes. Strain and reserve liquid. Remove and discard top shells and refrigerate mussels in the bottoms.

Sauté onions in olive oil over medium heat until soft and translucent, about 5 to 7 minutes. When onions are almost done, stir in garlic and sauté until soft and fragrant. Stir in bread crumbs, sun-dried tomatoes, lemon juice, oregano or marjoram, cayenne, if used, cooked filini, salt and pepper, and enough mussel liquid to make a firm stuffing.

Spoon about 1 tablespoon stuffing over each mussel; arrange mussels in a baking pan. Bake in a preheated oven (400°F/200°C/gas mark 6) until mussels are heated through and bread crumb topping is slightly toasted, about 10 to 12 minutes. Arrange on a serving platter and garnish with lemon wedges and oregano or marjoram sprigs. Serve hot.

To Drink: Any medium-bodied white or sparkling wine would be enjoyable — if you include the cayenne, choose a wine that's slightly sweet or very fruity to balance out the spice, or a good, medium-weight beer.

*Vermicelli with Smoked Whitefish, Pistachios and St. André

This sophisticated dish, with melt-in-the-mouth triple-crème St. André cheese and flecks of sweet smoked fish, makes an elegant first course or Sunday supper or an impressive center-piece for a brunch buffet. As a bonus, it's easy and quick to fix — and you can get all the sauce ingredients ready well in advance.

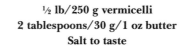

½ lb/250 g vermicelli
2 tablespoons/30 g/1 oz butter
Salt to taste

•

½ lb/250 g St. André cheese, at room temperature
¼ cup/60 mL/2 fl oz half-and-half (half milk, half cream)
¼ cup/60 mL/2 fl oz tart grapefruit juice
½ tablespoon finely minced grapefruit zest
¼ cup/45 g/1½ oz finely minced red (Spanish) onion
¼ cup/30 g/1 oz fresh parsley leaves, coarsely chopped
Salt to taste
½ teaspoon finely ground white or black pepper, or to taste

•

6 to 8 oz/185 to 250 g smoked whitefish or trout, boned and flaked
¼ cup/30 g/1 oz coarsely chopped pistachios
Parsley sprigs

Mash St. André cheese to a creamy consistency with half-and-half and grapefruit juice. Stir in grapefruit zest, onion, parsley, salt and pepper.

Cook the vermicelli (see page 10) about 5 minutes and toss with butter and salt, then with St. André mixture. Top with smoked whitefish, pistachios and parsley and serve hot or warm.

To Drink: The combination of butter and citrus in the pasta would be echoed deliciously by a big Chardonnay or a rich, fruity sparkling wine.

Clam-Stuffed Mushrooms

This surprisingly easy, yet supremely elegant appetizer teams huge, meaty mushrooms with a rich, creamy, clam-studded filling. You'll need a knife and fork — or lots of napkins!

1 oz stelline or other very small pasta, cooked (see page 10)

■

2 cans (6 oz/185 g) chopped clams (baby clams)
2 lb/1 kg jumbo mushrooms (about 12)
2 tablespoons olive oil
1 medium onion, finely chopped
2 cloves garlic, finely minced
¼ lb/120 g fresh shiitake, porcini or portobello mushrooms (or a combination), finely chopped
¼ cup/60 mL/2 fl oz cognac or brandy
¼ cup/60 mL/2 fl oz heavy (double) cream
¼ cup/30 g/1 oz fresh parsley leaves, coarsely chopped
Salt and freshly ground pepper to taste

Drain clams, reserving liquid for another use. Remove stems from jumbo mushrooms and wipe clean with a moist paper towel. Coat mushroom caps lightly with olive oil, using a pastry brush or paper towel, and set aside.

Sauté onions in butter over medium heat until soft and translucent, about 5 to 7 minutes. When onions are almost done, stir in garlic and sauté until soft and fragrant. Add chopped mushrooms; cover and cook until tender, about 5 minutes. Add cognac; light with a match and flambé, shaking pan until alcohol evaporates and flame goes out. Stir in cream and cook until liquid reduces slightly, about 2 to 3 minutes. Stir in parsley, clams and pasta. Adjust seasonings.

Spoon filling generously into mushroom caps and arrange stuffed mushrooms in a baking dish. Bake in a preheated oven (375°F/190°C/gas mark 5) until mushrooms are tender and filling is heated through, about 30 minutes. Serve hot.

To Drink: The cream and butter make this dish a natural match for a medium- to full-bodied Chardonnay, or a rich, sparkling wine or Champagne. Or try an earthy, light- to medium-bodied red such as a Pinot Noir to bring out the flavors of both kinds of mushrooms.

*Fettuccine with Smoked Salmon

This quick recipe pairs silken smoked salmon with such traditional partners as capers, red onion, lemon, sour cream and dill — as well as a not-so-traditional bed of fresh fettuccine. Try it for Sunday brunch instead of bagels and lox!

1 lb/500 g fresh fettuccine

•

¼ lb/120 g shallots, finely minced
4 tablespoons/60 g/2 oz butter
1 cup/250 mL/8 fl oz sour cream (crème fraîche)
½ cup/90 g/3 oz finely chopped red (Spanish) onion
½ cup/60 g/2 oz fresh dill, coarsely chopped
¼ cup/30 g/1 oz capers, drained
2 tablespoons lemon juice
½ tablespoon finely minced or grated lemon zest
½ teaspoon freshly ground white or black pepper
Salt to taste
½ lb/250 g smoked salmon, cut into strips (½ in/1.5 cm)

•

Thin strips of lemon zest or lemon wedges
Dill sprigs

Sauté shallots in butter over low-medium heat, stirring often, until soft and fragrant, about 5 to 7 minutes. Stir in remaining ingredients, except salmon, and warm through. Adjust seasonings.

Cook fettuccine (see page 10) about 2 minutes and toss with sauce. Transfer to a serving platter or individual bowls. Arrange salmon on top; garnish with lemon and dill. Serve hot.

To Drink: Rich, buttery flavors call for rich, full-flavored wines — try a toasty Chardonnay or a yeasty high-quality sparkler.

Lobster-Macadamia Wonton Ravioli

Ravioli made from scratch, with your own homemade dough, are wonderful, of course. But as I learned from the highly inventive Alan Wong of the Mauna Lani Bay Hotel on the Big Island of Hawaii, store-bought wonton wrappers, especially for East-West creations, make for a great shortcut. This sophisticated hors d'oeuvre brings a gingery Hawaiian lift to a traditional French hollandaise sauce. Chunks of buttery macadamia nuts in the filling echo the tropical theme.

2 to 3 dozen wonton wrappers,** 3 in/9 cm

Lobster-Macadamia Filling
2 cups/375 g/12 oz cooked lobster, crab or shrimp meat, or a combination, coarsely chopped
½ cup/60 g/2 oz macadamia nuts, coarsely chopped
2 green (spring) onions, thinly sliced (white plus 2 in/5 cm green)
2 tablespoons Shaohsing rice wine** or dry sherry
½ teaspoon salt

Ginger-Orange Hollandaise Sauce
6 egg yolks
¼ cup/60 mL/2 fl oz lemon juice
2 tablespoons orange juice concentrate
1½ tablespoons finely minced or grated orange zest
2 tablespoons fresh ginger juice (see page 140)
½ teaspoon salt, or to taste
½ teaspoon finely ground white pepper, or to taste
1 cup/250 g/8 oz butter, heated to bubbling

•

2 green (spring) onions, thinly sliced or cut in slivers (white plus 2 in/5 cm green)
½ orange, thinly sliced

For Lobster-Macadamia Filling: Combine all ingredients in a blender (liquidizer) or food processor and blend, using rapid pulses, until mixture is well blended but still slightly chunky.

For Ginger-Orange Hollandaise Sauce: Process egg yolks, lemon juice, orange juice and zest, ginger, salt and pepper at low speed in a blender or food processor until smooth. Slowly pour in hot butter and process until mixture is smooth and slightly thickened, about 15 seconds.

To fill wonton ravioli: Place a wonton wrapper on your work surface. (If wrappers are dusted on one side with flour to prevent sticking, place the powdery side down.) Center about 1 tablespoon filling on wonton wrapper. Moisten a ¼ in/.5 cm strip around edge of wonton with water; top with another wonton wrapper, powdery side up, and press firmly around edges.

Simmer wonton ravioli in water until firm-tender, about 5 to 7 minutes. Arrange on a serving platter or on individual plates. Top with Ginger-Orange Hollandaise Sauce and garnish with green onions and orange slices. Serve hot.

To Drink: The buttery, citrusy flavors of this dish would harmonize beautifully with a rich Chardonnay, or pop the cork on a festive sparkling wine.

**Available in Asian groceries or some supermarkets

Riso and Shrimp Grape Leaves

Greek stuffed grape leaves (dolmades) traditionally contain rice with various additions, such as lamb, pine nuts, currants or spices. In my version, the riso lends a slightly creamier texture and the egg-lemon (avgolemono) sauce makes a tangy counterpoint to the shrimp.

¼ lb/120 g riso or orzo, cooked (see page 10)

Shrimp Stuffing
1 medium onion, finely chopped
2 tablespoons/30 g/1 oz butter
2 tablespoons olive oil
4 cloves garlic, finely minced
¾ lb/375 g cooked shrimp meat, coarsely chopped
6 green (spring) onions, thinly sliced (white plus 2 in/5 cm green)
¼ cup/30 g/1 oz fresh parsley leaves, coarsely chopped
¼ cup/30 g/1 oz fresh mint leaves, finely minced
1 tablespoon finely minced or grated lemon zest
1 teaspoon salt, or to taste
½ teaspoon freshly ground pepper, or to taste

•

1 jar (8 oz/250 g) grape leaves (30 to 40 leaves)
¾ cup/185 mL/6 fl oz warm Fish Stock (see page 139), vegetable stock or water
2 tablespoons extra-virgin olive oil
¼ cup/60 mL/2 fl oz lemon juice

Avgolemono Sauce
3 eggs
1 tablespoon cornstarch (cornflour powder)
2 tablespoons lemon juice
p/250 mL/8 fl oz Fish Stock (see page 139) or vegetable
1 tablespoon finely minced fresh mint leaves
1 green (spring) onion, finely minced (white plus 2 in/5 cm green)
Salt and freshly ground pepper to taste

For Shrimp Stuffing: Sauté onion in butter and olive oil over medium heat until soft and translucent, about 5 to 7 minutes. When onions are almost done, stir in garlic and sauté until fragrant. Stir in the cooked riso, shrimp, green onions, parsley, mint, lemon zest, salt and pepper and mix well.

Drain and rinse grape leaves and stuff as follows: Place grape leaf in front of you, smooth side down and stem end toward you. Cut off stem. Place about 1 tablespoon filling near stem end and shape it into a horizontal log. Fold sides of leaf over filling, then fold stem end over and roll away from you so that the point of the leaf is on the outside.

Arrange stuffed grape leaves in an ovenproof pan. Pour in stock, olive oil and lemon juice. Cover pan and bake in a preheated oven (400°F/200°C/gas mark 6) until liquid is absorbed and grape leaves are heated through, about 30 to 40 minutes. Serve warm, chilled or at room temperature in a shallow bowl of Avgolemono Sauce, or use sauce as a dip.

For Avgolemono Sauce: Mix eggs, cornstarch and lemon juice in a small bowl. Heat stock to simmering and remove from heat. Stir about one-quarter of the stock into egg mixture, then slowly whisk egg mixture back into remaining stock. Simmer over very low heat, stirring constantly, until mixture thickens to the consistency of mayonnaise, about 3 to 5 minutes. Remove from heat; stir in mint and green onions and adjust seasonings. Serve warm or at room temperature.

To Drink: A Greek white wine; otherwise, any crisp, refreshing white will do nicely.

Mediterranean Baked Clams

Whenever I cook fresh clams, I wash and store away the largest shells so that, whenever I make these quick and easy appetizers, I can give them a fresh-from-the-sea flair even though I'm using canned clams. Store-bought scallop shells or small ramekins work well too.

1 oz/30 g pastina or other small pasta, cooked (see page 10)

∙

2 cans (6½ oz/185 g) chopped clams (baby clams), drained (reserve liquid)
6 cloves garlic, finely minced
2 green (spring) onions, thinly sliced (white plus 2 in/5 cm green)
⅓ cup/80 mL/3 fl oz olive oil
¼ cup/30 g/1 oz unseasoned bread crumbs
2 tablespoons pitted and finely chopped olives
(preferably a flavorful imported variety)
2 tablespoons capers
¼ cup/60 g/2 oz finely chopped fresh or canned tomato
¼ cup/45 g/1½ oz finely chopped red bell pepper (capsicum)
¼ cup/30 g/1 oz fresh basil leaves, coarsely chopped
¼ cup/30 g/1 oz fresh parsley leaves, coarsely chopped
½ teaspoon freshly ground pepper, or to taste
Salt to taste

∙

Lemon wedges, for garnish
Basil and parsley sprigs, for garnish

Combine all ingredients, including pastina, with enough reserved clam liquid to make a firm stuffing. Spoon into clam shells, scallop shells or small baking dishes. Bake in an oven preheated 400°F/200°C/gas mark 6 until cooked through and golden brown, about 20 to 30 minutes. Arrange on a serving platter and garnish with lemon wedges and herb sprigs. Serve hot.

To Drink: With the tangy Mediterranean flavors of this easy appetizer, an herbal Sauvignon Blanc would be a natural match.

Picnic Frittata

This year-round crowd-pleaser, great for picnics, potlucks or parties in a casual vein, flexes easily to take in whatever leftover pasta and vegetables you might have on hand. This quantity feeds at least a dozen.

½ lb/250 g mixed medium textured pasta, cooked (see page 10)

∎

¾ lb/375 g cooked small fresh or canned shrimp, drained

2 cups vegetables (raw grated carrots or zucchini (courgettes); fresh or frozen peas or corn; cooked asparagus, string (French green) beans or broccoli, or a combination

½ lb/250 g Jack (mild melting) cheese, grated

2 dozen eggs, beaten

½ cup/90 g/3 oz finely minced red (Spanish) onion

½ cup/60 g/2 oz fresh parsley leaves, coarsely chopped

1 teaspoon salt, or to taste

½ teaspoon freshly ground white or black pepper, or to taste

1 to 2 tablespoons chili powder, or to taste (optional)

Layer pasta, shrimp, vegetables and cheese in a nonstick baking pan. Combine eggs with remaining ingredients, pour over all and stir in gently.

Bake in a preheated oven (350°F/180°C/gas mark 4) until eggs are cooked through and firm, about 30 to 40 minutes. Refrigerate, cut into squares or wedges and serve warm, chilled or at room temperature.

To Drink: Don't fuss over beverages with this — a simple chilled beer or decent white jug wine wouldn't be out of place. To make it a bit more festive, pop open a few bottles of inexpensive Spanish cava sparkling wine.

*Spaghettini with Soft-Shell Crab

Soft-shell crabs, or "softies," are blue crabs (usually from the Chesapeake or Delaware Bays on the eastern American seaboard), caught while in the midst of a molt. Right after a softie sheds its hard outer shell, the undershell that remains is so tender you can eat the whole critter, shell and all. Enjoy them during their all-too-brief summer season.

½ lb/250 g spaghettini

•

4 soft-shell (blue) crabs

1 egg white, beaten

¼ cup/45 g/1½ oz all-purpose (plain) flour

½ cup/60 g/2 oz pecans, finely chopped

2 tablespoons/30 g/1 oz butter

2 tablespoons olive oil

¼ cup/60 mL/2 fl oz dry sherry

½ cup/60 mL/2 fl oz apple juice

2 tablespoons lemon juice

1 tablespoon finely minced or grated lemon zest

1 tablespoon fresh ginger juice (see page 140), optional

¼ cup/30 g/1 oz fresh parsley leaves, coarsely chopped

Salt and freshly ground pepper to taste

Dip soft-shell crabs in egg white, then dredge in flour. Sauté crab with pecans in butter and olive oil over medium-high heat until golden brown and cooked through, about 5 minutes per side. Stir in sherry and cook briefly to evaporate alcohol. Add remaining ingredients and cook, stirring, until liquid reduces slightly, about 2 to 3 minutes. Adjust seasonings.

About 5 minutes before the crabs are ready, cook spaghettini (see page 10) about 8 minutes. Toss with about three-quarters of the sauce; top with crab and remaining sauce. Serve hot.

To Drink: Given the sweet and spicy ingredients, a slightly sweet white or sparkling wine or a medium-weight malty beer would be your best bet.

Crab Stuffed Peppers

Fans of stuffed peppers will love this new twist on an old favorite. In the spicy-sweet double filling, a cheesy crab sauce melts into a mound of buttered tagliarine noodles. Assemble these a day ahead for a party, then just slip them into the oven when the doorbell rings.

½-¾ lb/250-375 g tagliarine, cooked (see page 10)
2 tablespoons/30 g/1 oz butter
¼ teaspoon salt, or to taste
•
6 large or 10 to 12 medium bell peppers (capsicums)
¾ lb/375 g crabmeat (or "imitation" crabmeat)
¼ lb/120 g Swiss (Gruyère) cheese, grated
⅓ cup/60 g/2 oz shredded or chopped carrot
¾ cup/120 g/4 oz corn kernels, fresh or frozen
4 green (spring) onions, thinly sliced (white plus 2 in/5 cm green)
¼ cup/60 mL/2 fl oz heavy (double) cream
¼ cup/60 mL/2 fl oz dry white wine
1 tablespoon lemon juice
½ teaspoon cayenne
Salt and freshly ground pepper to taste

Carefully cut a circle about 2 in/5 cm around the stem of each pepper. Leaving the peppers whole, remove and reserve stems; remove and discard seeds and inner membranes. Blanch peppers in boiling water for 5 minutes; drain.

Toss pasta with butter and salt. For each pepper, twirl a forkful of pasta into a "nest" and place into pepper, filling the bottom third. (Reserve any remaining pasta for another use.) Combine remaining ingredients and spoon evenly into peppers. Top with reserved stems. Arrange peppers in an ovenproof dish.

Bake peppers at 350°F/180°C/gas mark 4 for 45 minutes to 1 hour, depending on size of peppers. The peppers should be tender and juicy, the crab mixture hot and the cheese melted. Serve hot.

To Drink: Try a fruity or a slightly sweet white wine such as a Riesling or a Gewürztraminer to pick up the sweetness in this dish yet contrast its slight spice. Or experiment with a delicate red such as a light Pinot Noir.

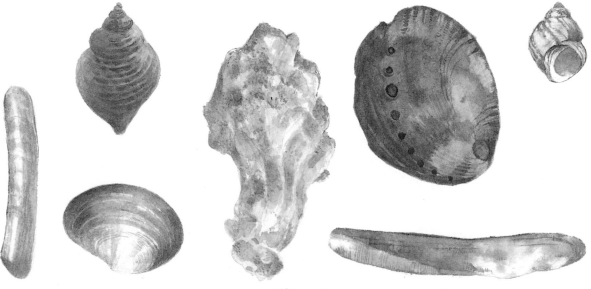

*Sushi-Seasoned Glass Noodle Rolls

Sushi purists might raise their eyebrows at this variation on their favorite snack, in which glass or bean thread noodles – made of ground mung beans – substitute for the usual rice. Give it a try, though: the flavors are very similar to the original, and the shimmery look and chewy feel of the noodles have an appeal all their own.

6 oz/185 g glass noodles

Sushi Seasoning
½ cup/120 ml/4 fl oz rice vinegar**
½ tablespoon sugar
1 teaspoon salt
3 green (spring) onions, thinly sliced (white plus 2 in/5 cm green)
▪
6 to 8 sheets nori seaweed**
⅓ lb/155 g raw hamachi (yellowtail), cut in thin strips
⅓ lb/155 g raw maguro (lean tuna), cut in thin strips
▪
Soy sauce
Wasabi** (Japanese horseradish)
Japanese-style pickled ginger**

Soak glass noodles in hot water until softened but not gluey (about 2 to 5 minutes depending on thickness of noodle and temperature of water); drain well. Combine ingredients for sushi seasoning in a small bowl. Toss glass noodles with sushi seasoning.

Place a sheet of nori, shiny side down, on a bamboo sushi-rolling mat or square of plastic wrap (cling film). Spread a thin layer of glass noodles on nori, leaving a strip (1 in/2.5 cm) of the edge furthest away from you uncovered. Place a few strips of hamachi and maguro horizontally along the front edge. Roll the nori away from you and press edge firmly to seal the roll. Slice the roll with a very sharp knife into 4 to 6 pieces. Serve with soy sauce and wasabi, mixed to taste as a dip, and pickled ginger.

Variation: For cone-shaped hand rolls (temaki), halve sheets of nori. With one long edge of nori toward you, arrange noodles and fish diagonally across nori from center of bottom edge to left corner of top edge. Fold bottom left corner of nori over filling and wrap right edge around to form a cone. Serve as above.

To Drink: Beer and sake are traditional with sushi, but feel free to experiment with fruity, slightly sweet white or sparkling wines.

**Available in Asian groceries or some supermarkets

Crispy Shrimp Wontons

This savory appetizer started out as a seafood variation on the theme of green onion pancakes, but soon took on a life of its own — and a whole new shape. You can mix the filling several hours in advance, stuff the wonton triangles just before your guests arrive and fry them up just before serving.

4 to 5 dozen wonton wrappers**

•

Water or 1 egg white, beaten

Shrimp-Shiitake Filling

¹⁄₂ lb/120 g cooked bay shrimp, coarsely chopped

4 green (spring) onions, thinly sliced (white plus 2 in/5 cm green)

¹⁄₄ lb/120 g fresh shiitake mushrooms,** finely chopped

¹⁄₄ cup/45 g/1¹⁄₂ oz oil-packed sun-dried tomatoes, drained and finely chopped

2 tablespoons capers, finely chopped

1 tablespoon sesame oil**

1 tablespoon fresh ginger juice (see p. 140)

¹⁄₂ teaspoon chili oil,** or to taste

•

about 3 cups/750 mL/24 fl oz olive oil

about 3 cups/750 mL/24 fl oz vegetable oil

Soy sauce

Rice vinegar

Combine all ingredients for filling in a small bowl. Place a wonton wrapper on your work surface. (If wrappers are dusted on one side with flour to prevent sticking, place the powdery side down.) Moisten a ¹⁄₄ in/.5 cm strip around the edge with water or egg white. Center about ¹⁄₂ tablespoon of the filling on the wonton wrapper and fold wrapper in half diagonally, forming a triangle. Press gently to squeeze out air, and press down firmly around edges to seal.

Combine olive and vegetable oils in a pan to a depth of 1 in/2.5 cm and heat to 400°F/200°C/gas mark 6. Fry wonton triangles, a few at a time and turning once, until crisp and golden, about 2 minutes per side. (You may need to add more oil halfway through.) Serve hot with a bowl of soy sauce mixed with rice vinegar for dipping.

To Drink: Because the shiitake mushrooms and sun-dried tomatoes add a lot of intensity to this dish, you can serve a light-bodied red — or stick with a fruity, slightly sweet white, a full-flavored sparkling wine or a rich, malty beer.

**Available in Asian groceries or some supermarkets

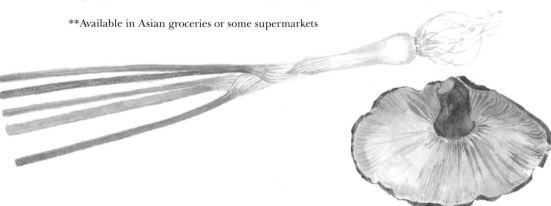

Seafood Potstickers with Minted Mango Salsa

Although the familiar Chinese restaurant potsticker usually contains a pork filling, seafood makes a lighter, fresher-tasting alternative. The mint-flecked mango salsa makes this delectable appetizer lighter and fresher still.

30 to 40 round potsticker, shao-mai or gyoza wrappers**

Minted Mango Salsa
¼ cup/60 mL/2 fl oz rice vinegar or lime juice, or 2 tablespoons of each**
1 medium mango, cut into cubes (½ in/1.5 cm)
2 green (spring) onions, thinly sliced (white plus 2 in/5 cm green)
2 tablespoons thinly sliced fresh mint leaves
½ to 1 small fresh hot red chile (or to taste), very finely minced
Salt to taste

Potsticker Filling
½ lb/250 g raw shrimp or prawns, peeled and deveined
½ lb/250 g rockfish fillet, or other mild white fish
1 egg white
1 tablespoon sesame oil**
½ cup/60 g/2 oz fresh cilantro (coriander) leaves, coarsely chopped
4 green (spring) onions, thinly sliced (white plus 2 in/5 cm green)
2 cloves garlic, finely minced
1 tablespoon fresh ginger juice (see page 140), optional
½ teaspoon salt
·
¼ cup/60 mL/2 fl oz peanut or other vegetable oil
2 cups/500 mL/16 fl oz Fish Stock (see page 139)

For Minted Mango Salsa: Combine all ingredients in a small bowl; allow flavors to blend at least ½ hour.

For potstickers: Combine all filling ingredients in a food processor and blend, using short, rapid pulses, until mixture is well blended but still slightly chunky.

Place a potsticker wrapper on your work surface and spoon ¾ to 1 tablespoon filling into center of wrapper. (If wrappers are dusted on one side with flour to prevent sticking, place the powdery side down.) Moisten a strip ¼ in/.5 cm along edge of wrapper with water and fold wrapper in half over filling. Pinch the potsticker closed and, holding it vertically, flatten the base on your work surface.

Heat half the oil over medium-high heat; add half the potstickers and pan-fry until the flattened base is lightly browned, 30 seconds to 1 minute. Add half the fish stock, cover and cook over medium-high heat until stock is absorbed and noodle wrappers are tender, about 10 minutes. (Add more stock if necessary to finish cooking potstickers.) Uncover pan and continue cooking until flattened base is crisp and brown, about 2 to 3 minutes. Repeat with remaining potstickers (or use 2 pans simultaneously). Serve hot with Minted Mango Salsa.

To Drink: For spicy-sweet East-West combos such as this, try fruity, off-dry white wines, slightly sweet sparkling wines or ice-cold beer.

**Available in Asian groceries or some supermarkets

*Green-Tea Soba with Tamari-Ginger Sauce

This dish of buckwheat noodles makes a very refreshing summer lunch or a light lead-in to a multi-course Japanese dinner. And with bright orange carrot, pale green onion, pure white daikon and sliced fish cake edged in neon pink, it wakes up the eye as well as the palate.

½ lb/250 g green-tea or regular soba**

Tamari-Ginger Sauce:
¼ cup/60 mL/2 fl oz tamari** (wheat-free soy sauce)
2 tablespoons rice vinegar**
1 tablespoon sesame oil**
1 tablespoon finely minced Japanese-style pickled ginger** or
fresh ginger juice (see page 140), optional
2 green (spring) onions, thinly sliced (white plus 2 in/5 cm green)
∙
1 cup/90 g/3 oz grated carrot (1 medium carrot)
1 cup/90 g/3 oz grated daikon** (Japanese radish)
4-6 oz/120-185 g packaged fish cake (kamaboko),** thinly sliced

Stir soba into boiling water. When water comes to a boil again, add 1 cup cold water, stir and bring to a boil again. Repeat a third time. Turn off heat, cover pot and let stand 10 minutes. Rinse noodles with cold water and drain well.

Combine ingredients for Tamari-Ginger Sauce. Toss noodles with half the sauce and chill thoroughly. Divide noodles among individual bowls and top with carrot, daikon and fish cake. Spoon remaining tamari sauce over all and serve chilled.

To Drink: Relax and enjoy a really cold beer or a simple, slightly sweet white or sparkling wine.

**Available in Asian groceries or some supermarkets

Tilapia Spring Rolls

Fans of catfish will love tilapia, a freshwater fish found throughout Southeast Asia that is now being successfully farm-raised elsewhere. If you prefer the flavor of saltwater fish, substitute rockfish, snapper, shrimp or a combination. And by the way, an extra pair of hands can help speed this dish along — just divide up the tasks of soaking the rice paper, filling the spring rolls and managing the fry pan.

15 to 20 rice paper circles,** 8½ in/21 cm diameter
Warm water

Dipping Sauce
2 cloves garlic, finely minced
2 tablespoons soy sauce
2 tablespoons lime juice
2 tablespoons fish sauce** (nuoc mam or nam pla)
2 tablespoons hoisin sauce**
1 to 2 tablespoons chili sauce,** or to taste
1 tablespoon finely minced fresh mint leaves
1 tablespoon green (spring) onion, thinly sliced (green part only)
½ tablespoon finely minced fresh cilantro (coriander) leaves

Filling
¾ lb/375 g tilapia or other mild white fish fillets, cut into strips (½ in/1.5 cm)
1 cup/120 g/4 oz bean sprouts
¼ cup/45 g/1½ oz finely grated carrot
¼ cup/60 mL/2 fl oz lime juice
2 tablespoons fresh mint leaves, finely minced
2 tablespoons fresh cilantro (coriander) leaves, finely minced
2 green (spring) onions, thinly sliced (white plus 2 in/5 cm green)
1 tablespoon finely minced lime zest
½ small fresh hot chile, finely minced (about ½ tablespoon), or to taste
2 cups/500 mL/16 fl oz vegetable oil
•
1 small head butter lettuce, separated (at least 15 to 20 leaves)
Mint leaves
Cilantro (coriander) leaves

Combine ingredients for dipping sauce and let stand 1 hour or more to blend flavors.

Combine ingredients for filling in a small bowl. Soak rice paper circles in hot water, one at a time, until pliable but still intact, about 1 to 2 minutes. Place about 2 tablespoons filling just below center of each rice paper circle; fold over sides and roll up from bottom. Heat vegetable oil to 375°F/190°C/gas mark 5 and fry spring rolls a few at a time.

Arrange on lettuce leaves on a small serving plate and serve with dipping sauce. Garnish with mint and cilantro. To eat, wrap a spring roll, along with some mint and cilantro leaves, in a lettuce leaf and dip in sauce.

To Drink: A beer, a fruity white wine or sparkler, or a slightly herbal Sauvignon Blanc will do nicely here.

**Available in Asian groceries or some supermarkets

Pasta Pissaladière

*The Provençal town of Nice boasts among its regional specialties a savory tart called
pissaladière. Thick with slow-cooked, caramelized onions, olives and a lacing of
anchovy paste, my version is made with layers of easy-cooking lasagne noodles instead of
a pizza-like dough.*

½ lb/250 g lasagne noodles, cooked (see page 10)
2 tablespoons olive oil
Salt to taste

▪

4 medium onions, thinly sliced
¼ cup/60 mL/2 fl oz olive oil
1 tablespoon finely minced fresh rosemary
1 teaspoon freshly ground pepper, or to taste
Salt to taste
⅓ cup/60 g/2 oz freshly grated parmesan cheese
¼ cup/30 g/1 oz pitted, halved Niçoise or other flavorful olives
1 can (2 oz/60 g) anchovy fillets, drained and halved lengthwise

Sauté onions in olive oil over low-medium heat, stirring frequently, until caramelized and golden, about 45 minutes to 1 hour. Stir in rosemary, pepper and salt.

Toss lasagne noodles with olive oil and salt and layer them in a shallow oblong baking dish, using half the noodles, half the onion mixture and half the parmesan first, then the remaining noodles, onions and parmesan. Arrange olives and anchovies on top in an attractive crisscross pattern.

Bake, uncovered, in a preheated oven 375°F/190°C/gas mark 5 until heated through and slightly golden, about 15 minutes. Cut into squares and serve at any temperature.

To Drink: A full-bodied dry white wine or light red would work nicely, but a good-quality sparkling wine would especially complement the salty anchovies.

Riso Risotto with Clams

True risotto, made with a special, sticky rice that must be slowly and carefully cooked, is a mainstay of Italy's northern provinces. You can speed up the process, without sacrificing flavor, by using rice-shaped riso or orzo pasta instead.

1 lb/500 g riso or orzo

·

4 dozen small littleneck or Manila clams (about 3 lb/1.5 kg)
1 cup/250 mL/8 fl oz white wine
About 1½ cups/375 mL/12 fl oz Fish Stock (see page 139) or clam broth, warmed
2 medium onions, finely chopped
¼ cup/60 mL/2 fl oz olive oil
2 tablespoons/30 g/1 oz butter
4 cloves garlic, finely minced
1 medium yellow bell pepper (capsicum), finely diced
1 medium carrot, finely diced
1 cup/155 g/5 oz fresh or frozen green peas
¼ cup/30 g/1 oz fresh parsley, coarsely chopped
½ tablespoon fresh thyme leaves
Salt and freshly ground pepper to taste

Steam clams with wine until shells open. Remove clams and strain liquid into a measure. Add enough Fish Stock to equal 2 cups/500 mL/16 fl oz and reserve.

Cook riso (see page 10) for about 8 minutes. Meanwhile, sauté onions in olive oil and butter over medium heat until soft, about 5 to 7 minutes. When onions are almost done, stir in garlic, yellow pepper and carrots and sauté until garlic is fragrant. Stir in peas and reserved clam liquid. Simmer 2 to 3 minutes, or until peas are crisp-tender. Stir in riso, parsley and thyme; heat through. If mixture seems too dry, stir in more stock. Adjust seasonings. Divide among individual bowls; top with clams and serve hot.

To Drink: You'll need a rather delicate white here — try an Italian Soave or Verdicchio or a slightly herbal Sauvignon Blanc.

*Hazelnut~Vanilla Oysters

Rich, savory and sensuous, this dish is ideal as a first course or a luncheon entree. Although vanilla may seem an unusual ingredient in a main dish, its warm, appealing flavor can make a sauce taste smoother and creamier. It also brings out the natural sweetness in fish and shellfish. Taste this butter sauce before and after adding the vanilla — you'll see what a difference it makes!

1 lb/500 g capelli d'angelo "nests"

•

1 jar (10 oz/000 g) oysters, or 1 to 1½ dozen fresh oysters, shucked
½ cup/60 g/2 oz toasted hazelnuts (see page 141), finely chopped
¼ cup/15 g/½ oz fine-textured unseasoned bread crumbs
1 egg white, beaten

•

2 tablespoons olive oil
4 tablespoons/60 g/2 oz butter
½ cup/120 mL/4 fl oz dry white wine, preferably a rich Chardonnay
1 cup/250 mL/8 fl oz Fish Stock (see page 139)
1 tablespoon lemon juice
½ tablespoon finely minced lemon zest
¼ cup/60 mL/2 fl oz heavy (double) cream
¼ cup/30 g/1 oz fresh parsley leaves, coarsely chopped
½ teaspoon vanilla
Salt and freshly ground pepper to taste

•

Lemon slices or wedges
Parsley sprigs

Drain and reserve oyster liquor. Combine hazelnuts and bread crumbs. Dip oysters in egg white, then in bread crumb mixture, patting crumb mixture on firmly and coating oysters thoroughly.

In a wide skillet, heat olive oil and butter over medium heat until mixture begins to sizzle. Sauté the oysters, shaking pan frequently. Turn oysters once, cooking until coating is golden brown, about 1 to 2 minutes per side. Remove oysters and keep warm.

Add wine, Fish Stock and reserved oyster liquor to skillet and cook until liquid reduces by about half. Stir in lemon juice and zest, cream, parsley, vanilla and oysters; heat through. Adjust seasonings.

Cook capelli d'angelo, about 5 minutes, and drain carefully to keep "nests" intact (see page 10). Arrange nests on a serving platter or individual plates. Divide oysters among nests, spooning sauce evenly over pasta to coat completely. Garnish with lemon and parsley and serve hot.

To Drink: My favorite wine with this dish is a big, rich Chardonnay, with toasty, buttery qualities. Oak aging will give the wine a vanilla-like taste. With so many flavors in the dish matching the same flavors in the wine, the two work together extremely well. (Just make sure that the wine has enough acidity to cut through the creamy sauce as you drink it, just as a squeeze of lemon would.)

Calamari Stuffed with Shrimp and Orzo

Calamari, or squid, make perfect natural casings for all types of savory stuffings. In this Mediterranean recipe, they contain shrimp, sun-dried tomatoes and nuggets of orzo pasta. You can choose between pungent green peppercorns and salt-tangy capers to spark the tomato-rich sauce.

3 oz/90 g orzo or riso, cooked (see page 10)

Stuffing
½ lb/250 g small cooked bay shrimp
⅓ cup/60 g/2 oz finely chopped sun-dried tomatoes
4 green (spring) onions, thinly sliced (white plus 2 in/5 cm green)
Salt and freshly ground pepper to taste
2 lb/1 kg medium to large calamari (squid), cleaned and left whole (reserve tentacles for another use or bake alongside stuffed calamari)

Tomato-Olive Sauce
2 medium onions, finely chopped
¼ cup/60 mL/2 fl oz olive oil
4 cloves garlic, finely minced
½ cup/120 mL/4 fl oz dry white wine
2 cups/500 g/1 lb finely chopped fresh or canned tomatoes
½ cup/45 g/1½ oz quartered pitted green olives
2 tablespoons green peppercorns or capers
¼ cup/30 g/1 oz fresh parsley leaves, coarsely chopped
2 tablespoons fresh oregano or marjoram leaves
Salt and freshly ground pepper to taste

Combine ingredients for stuffing with cooked orzo and stuff calamari loosely, using a spoon or a pastry bag without a tip. Close calamari by threading the opening with a toothpick.

For Tomato-Olive Sauce: Sauté onions in olive oil over medium heat until soft and translucent, about 5 to 7 minutes. When onions are almost done, stir in garlic and sauté until soft and fragrant. Stir in wine, tomatoes, olives and green peppercorns or capers and simmer 20 minutes, stirring occasionally. Stir in parsley and oregano and adjust seasonings.

Cover the bottom of a baking dish with sauce. Arrange stuffed calamari in baking dish and top with remaining sauce. Bake, covered, in a preheated oven (375°F/190°C/gas mark 5) until calamari are tender, about 15 to 20 minutes. Serve hot.

To Drink: A tart, full-flavored white or sparkling wine, or even a light, chillable red, stands up nicely to the meaty calamari and their zesty sauce.

*Saracen Spaghettini

The Arabic culinary influence of Saracen seafarers shows up frequently throughout Italy wherever main dishes call for sweet ingredients such as raisins. The sautéed bread crumbs are a typical Sicilian touch.

1 lb/500 g spaghettini

•

8 cloves garlic, finely minced
½ cup/120 mL/4 fl oz olive oil, divided
1 can (2 oz/60 g) anchovy fillets, finely chopped or mashed
½ cup/120 mL/4 fl oz dry white wine
½ cup/120 mL/4 fl oz Fish Stock (see page 139)
⅓ cup/60 g/2 oz raisins (golden raisins (sultanas), if available)
⅓ cup/60 g/2 oz oil-packed sun-dried tomatoes, drained and coarsely chopped
½ cup/60 g/2 oz fresh parsley leaves, coarsely chopped
⅓ cup/45 g/1½ oz pine nuts (kernels)
⅓ cup/20 g/¾ oz unseasoned bread crumbs
Salt and freshly ground pepper to taste

Cook the spaghettini (see page 10) about 8 minutes.

Meanwhile, sauté garlic in half the olive oil over medium heat, stirring frequently, until it turns fragrant and golden but does not burn, about 3 to 5 minutes. Add anchovies, mashing until they dissolve. Add wine and cook until liquid reduces by one-third, about 2 minutes. Stir in Fish Stock, raisins, sun-dried tomatoes and parsley and simmer 1 to 2 minutes to blend flavors. Adjust seasonings.

In a separate pan, sauté pine nuts and bread crumbs in remaining olive oil over medium heat until golden brown, about 3 minutes.

Toss spaghettini with anchovy mixture and transfer to a serving platter. Sprinkle with pine nuts and bread crumbs and serve hot.

To Drink: This dish can work with either a medium-bodied white wine with good acidity or a fruity, relatively light red sparkling wine.

Gnocchi with Clams and Parsley-Chèvre Pesto

Goat cheese, also called by its French name, chèvre, is tangier and lower in fat than most cow's milk cheeses. Although some find the chewy texture of gnocchi (NYOH-kee) an acquired taste, these little flour-and-potato dumplings have their staunch devotees. Do try making your own gnocchi at least once - but when you're pressed for time, the commercial products substitute well.

1 lb/500 g potato gnocchi, preferably homemade (see page 11)

Gnocchi
2 lb/1 kg potatoes (preferably old, dry and starchy)
2 cups/315 g/10 oz all-purpose (plain) flour
½ tablespoon salt

Parsley-Chèvre Pesto
2 cups/250 g/8 oz fresh parsley leaves
¼ lb/120 g creamy chèvre (goat cheese)
2 tablespoons pine nuts (kernels) or walnuts
2 tablespoons lemon juice
4 to 6 cloves garlic, or to taste
¼ cup/60 mL/2 fl oz olive oil
▪
2 (6 oz/18 g) cans chopped clams (baby clams)
Salt and freshly ground pepper to taste

For Gnocchi: Steam potatoes over boiling water until soft enough to pierce easily with a fork. Peel when just cool enough to handle. Combine flour and salt and begin mashing potatoes while still warm, mixing flour in gradually until completely incorporated.

Break off small lumps of the dough and roll them out into long logs (about ¾ in/ 2 cm). Slice these into lengths 1 in/2.5 cm. Sprinkle with flour at any stage if dough seems sticky. Using three fingers or the palm of your hand, roll the gnocchi one by one on a cheese grater (the prickly surface textures the gnocchi so they cook faster and hold sauce better) into a rounded oval shape. Cook the homemade or purchased gnocchi in a large pot of barely boiling water until it floats to the surface, about 3 to 4 minutes.

Combine all ingredients for Parsley-Chèvre Pesto in a blender (liquidizer) or food processor and process to a smooth paste. Transfer to a saucepan; stir in clams and their liquid and heat through. Adjust seasonings.

Toss gnocchi with about three-quarters of the sauce; top with remaining sauce and serve hot.

To Drink: To match the tang of the goat cheese and lemon, choose a pleasantly tart, medium-bodied white. California's pioneering goat cheese producer Laura Chenel's first choice, and mine, would be Sauvignon Blanc.

*California Rice Paper Rolls

Rice paper, a staple of Southeast Asia, comes packaged in thin, brittle circles that turn pliable and tender when you soak them in hot water. These quick, easy, no-cook appetizers are a rice paper version of the popular "California roll" sushi made with rice, a seaweed wrapper and traditional Japanese accompaniments. If you can find them, use shiso leaves for a fresh lemony herbal taste. This relative of basil and mint, also called beefsteak plant or perilla, refreshes and cleanses the palate.

4 rice paper circles,** 8½ in/21 cm diameter

·

⅓ lb/155 g fresh crabmeat or imitation crab (also called kani kamaboko**)
1 medium avocado, peeled, seeded and thinly sliced
¼ medium cucumber, cut into thin sticks
2 green (spring) onions, quartered lengthwise

Optional
Daikon (Japanese radish) sprouts**
Green shiso leaves,** slivered
Japanese-style pickled ginger,** coarsely chopped

·

Soy sauce
Wasabi paste or wasabi powder,** mixed with water
Juice from Japanese-style pickled ginger**

Soak rice paper circles in hot water, one at a time, until pliable but still intact, 1 to 2 minutes. Spread rice paper out carefully on work surface. Arrange crab in a horizontal strip, slightly below center, leaving about 1 in/2.5 cm of rice paper uncovered on each side. Top crab with avocado, cucumber, green onions and optional ingredients if used. Fold sides of rice paper over filling. Fold bottom of rice paper over filling and roll away from you into a log shape. Slice each log into 4 pieces. Chill and serve cold, with small individual dishes for each diner to custom-blend a dipping sauce of soy, wasabi and ginger juice.

To Drink: At a sushi bar, beer or sake would be the usual choices — but try a light, fruity white or sparkling wine, if you prefer.

**Available in Asian groceries or some supermarkets

*East-West Tuna Tartare

Inspired by steak tartare, with flavors from both Eastern and Western traditions, this easy hors d'oeuvre is a great introduction to the succulence of raw fish.

2 dozen wonton wrappers, halved or quartered if desired
4 cups/1 L/32 fl oz peanut or vegetable oil

■

½ lb/250 g ahi tuna, coarsely chopped
2 anchovy fillets, finely chopped or mashed
2 cloves garlic, very finely minced
2 tablespoons finely minced Japanese-style pickled ginger or 1 tablespoon
fresh ginger juice (see page 140)
2 green (spring) onions, very thinly sliced (white plus 2 in/5 cm green)
¼ cup/30 g/1 oz fresh cilantro (coriander) leaves, coarsely chopped
2 tablespoons capers
½ tablespoon sesame oil**
½ tablespoon soy sauce
1 teaspoon wasabi powder, or to taste

Fry wonton wrappers at 400°F/200°C/gas mark 6 in peanut or vegetable oil until crisp and golden, about 1 minute per side. (The noodles will puff up as they cook.)

Using two forks, mix tuna with remaining ingredients. Serve chilled as a dip or spread for wonton chips.

To Drink: To offset the spice, try a slightly sweet white wine or a light, fruity red. A sparkling wine will also pick up the toastiness of the crisp-fried noodles.

**Available in Asian groceries or some supermarkets

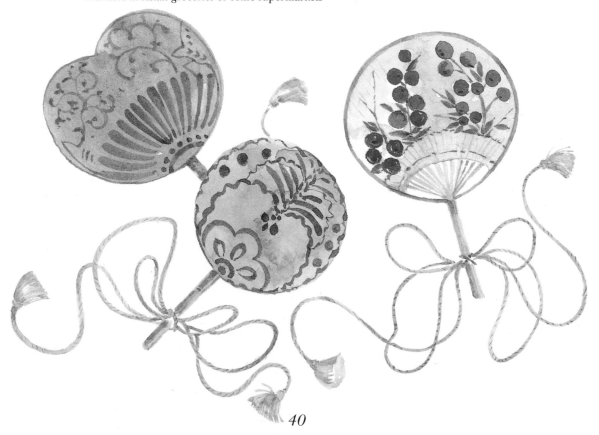

*Unagi with Soba and Ponzu-Citrus Sauce

This easy yet exotic recipe showcases the rich taste and unctuous texture of broiled Japanese-style eel against a backdrop of buckwheat noodles. Asian markets carry it in the freezer case, usually with a packet of sweet sauce tucked into the wrapping. Sansho, related to Szechwan peppercorns but not true pepper, adds a fresh, citrusy lift. If you can't find ponzu sauce, which is simply citrus-flavored soy sauce, you can make your own very easily.

½ lb/250 g soba,** cooked as directed on package or on page 10

Ponzu-Citrus Sauce

¼ cup/60 mL/2 fl oz ponzu sauce** or 2 tablespoons each soy sauce
and lemon juice

2 tablespoons tangerine or orange juice

2 tablespoons lemon juice

4 green (spring) onions, thinly sliced (white plus 2 in/5 cm green)

2 tablespoons fresh ginger juice (see page 140)

1 tablespoon grated tangerine or orange zest

1 teaspoon powdered sansho** (optional)

Sauce packet from frozen unagi**

•

1 package (5 oz/150 g) frozen unagi (eel), with sauce packet,** thawed

Mix ingredients for Ponzu-Citrus Sauce, including sauce packet from unagi, and set aside. Heat unagi briefly in a conventional or microwave oven. Place soba in a serving bowl or soup tureen or divide among individual bowls. Spoon Ponzu-Citrus Sauce over soba and top with unagi. Serve hot.

To Drink: The classic drinks here would be warmed sake or cold beer. Or try an off-dry white or sparkling wine or a fruity red instead.

**Available in Asian groceries or some supermarkets

41

Steamed Shrimp Dumplings with Spicy Cilantro Vinaigrette

These bite-sized, ruffle-edged morsels make a wonderful lead-in to any Chinese dinner or feature in a dim sum feast of "little treasures." The wrapping technique is, happily, easier to do than to describe: after spooning a dollop of filling in the center of the wrapper, firmly pinch the wrapper together at 12 o'clock and 6 o'clock with the thumb and forefinger of one hand, and at 3 o'clock and 9 o'clock with the thumb and forefinger of the other. Repeat this step with the four arcs of dough that are left sticking out for a lovely scalloped effect. You'll get the hang of it in no time!

30 to 40 shao-mai or gyoza wrappers** (about 6 oz/185 g)

Spicy Cilantro Vinaigrette
2 tablespoons rice vinegar**
2 tablespoons soy sauce
1 tablespoon sesame oil**
½ teaspoon chili oil,** or to taste
2 cloves garlic, very finely minced
2 tablespoons fresh cilantro (coriander) leaves, finely minced
½ teaspoon fresh ginger juice (see page 140)

Shrimp and Waterchestnut Filling
1 lb/500 g raw shrimp or prawns, peeled and deveined
1 cup/155 g/5 oz waterchestnuts, fresh or canned**
¼ lb/120 g fresh shiitake mushrooms** (or 6 dried, reconstituted in water)
2 green (spring) onions, thinly sliced (white plus 2 in/5 cm green)
½ cup/60 g/2 oz fresh cilantro (coriander) leaves
2 tablespoons slivered almonds
2 tablespoons Shaohsing rice wine** or dry sherry
1 tablespoon sesame oil**
1 tablespoon soy sauce

For Spicy Cilantro Vinaigrette: Whisk ingredients together in a small bowl; allow flavors to blend at least ½ hour.

For Shrimp and Waterchestnut Filling: Coarsely chop shrimp, waterchestnuts and shiitake mushrooms. Place in a food processor with remaining filling ingredients and blend, using short, rapid pulses, until mixture is well blended but still slightly chunky.

To prepare dumplings: Spoon ¾ to 1 tablespoon of filling into center of each wrapper. (If wrappers are dusted on one side with flour, place the powdery side down.) Fold wrapper around filling, pinching on four opposite sides, then in between, as described above. Arrange dumplings on oiled steaming rack over pan of boiling water. (Don't crowd them or they might stick together.) Cover and steam gently until wrappers are firm-tender and filling is cooked through, about 10 to 12 minutes. Serve at any temperature with Spicy Cilantro Vinaigrette.

Note: If all you have are square rather than round wonton wrappers, you can round off the corners with a knife or scissors.

To Drink: With all this spice, reach for a frosty, light- to medium-weight beer. Wine lovers can try a slightly sweet Gewürztraminer, Riesling, Chenin Blanc or white Zinfandel or an inexpensive sparkler such as Spanish cava instead.

**Available in Asian groceries or some supermarkets

Crayfish with Apricot-Orange Butter

Dubbed crawfish in the American South and yabbies in Australia, these freshwater lobsters-in-miniature have earned a loyal following in both hemispheres. Whatever you call them, enjoy them to the fullest by breaking them apart, nibbling out the tender tail meat and sucking the rich nugget of fat from the head. Feel free to adjust the spices to your own taste (and if you can't get live crayfish, feel free to use prawns instead).

½ lb/250 g orzo or riso

•

3 lb/1.5 kg live crayfish or 1¼ lb/620 g prawns, deveined but not shelled
6 to 8 garlic cloves, finely minced
¼ cup/60 g/2 oz butter
2 tablespoons olive or other vegetable oil
1 cup/250 mL/8 fl oz beer
¼ cup/45 g/1½ oz finely minced dried apricots
2 tablespoons lemon juice
2 tablespoons orange juice concentrate
½ to 1 teaspoon cumin
½ to 1 teaspoon allspice
¼ to ½ teaspoon cayenne, or to taste
¼ cup/30 g/1 oz fresh parsley leaves, coarsely chopped
½ teaspoon freshly ground white or black pepper, or to taste
Salt to taste

Soak crayfish in several changes of water for 30 minutes to 1 hour to wash away mud and sand. Blanch crayfish in boiling water until shells turn red, 30 seconds to 1 minute. Drain crayfish. (If using prawns, this is not necessary.)

Sauté garlic in butter and olive oil over medium-high heat, stirring often, until soft and fragrant, about 2 to 3 minutes. Stir in crayfish or prawns and coat evenly. Add beer, apricots, lemon juice, orange juice concentrate, cumin, allspice and cayenne; simmer 8 to 10 minutes, stirring frequently. Add parsley and adjust seasonings.

While the sauce is simmering, cook orzo (see page 10) about 8 minutes. Mound on a serving platter; surround with crayfish and top with sauce. Serve hot.

To Drink: Both quite sweet and mildly spicy, this dish works best with a medium-weight beer or a slightly sweet white or sparkling wine.

*Aglio e Olio with Smoked Trout

When the cupboard is just about bare, a simple aglio e olio (garlic and oil) pasta can make a quick and satisfying meal. Spiff it up with some sweet, juicy smoked trout for an elegant brunch or after-theater supper — and feel free to experiment with other seafood such as smoked salmon or sturgeon, leftover cooked fish, or canned tuna, sardines or anchovies.

½ lb/250 g spaghettini
∙
8 cloves garlic, finely minced
⅓ cup/80 mL/3 fl oz olive oil
¼ cup/30 g/1 oz thinly sliced green (spring) onions, green part only
¼ cup/30 g/1 oz fresh parsley leaves, coarsely chopped
¼ cup/45 g/1½ oz grated parmesan cheese
Salt and freshly ground white or black pepper to taste
½ lb/250 g smoked trout, bones removed, flaked or thinly sliced

Cook the spaghettini (see page 10) about 8 minutes.

Meanwhile, sauté garlic in olive oil over low-medium heat, stirring often, until soft and fragrant, about 5 to 7 minutes. Toss with spaghettini; add green onions, parsley and parmesan and toss again. Adjust seasonings. Transfer to a serving platter and top with smoked trout. Serve hot.

To Drink: Smoked fish automatically brings sparkling wine to mind — or choose a crisp Italian or California white.

*Vermicelli with Caviar

Caviar — snack food of the czars; the height of luxury for us mere mortals. Although purists insist on serving it with nothing more than a spoon, caviar teams classically with onions, sour cream, hard-boiled eggs and blini. Why not delicate vermicelli pasta instead, which makes life so much easier?

½ lb/250 g vermicelli

▪

2 tablespoons/30 g/1 oz melted butter
¼ cup/60 mL/2 fl oz heavy (double) cream warmed
¼ cup/15 g/½ oz finely minced fresh chives, divided
2 tablespoons finely minced red (Spanish) onion
Salt and freshly ground white pepper to taste
¼ cup/60 mL/2 fl oz sour cream (crème fraîche)
1 hard-boiled egg, sieved or finely minced
1 oz/30 g caviar, preferably imported beluga, sevruga or osetra

Cook the vermicelli (see page 10) about 5 minutes. Toss with butter, cream, half the chives, the red onion, salt and pepper. Place on a serving platter or divide among individual bowls. Top with sour cream, remaining chives, hard-boiled egg and caviar. Serve hot.

To Drink: Caviar and champagne — luxury on top of luxury! Enjoy the tiny bubbles of both as they pop, pop, pop in your mouth.

Mediterranean Stuffed Peppers

In this great party dish, peppers are halved lengthwise into "boats" and filled with a piquant, palate-teasing stuffing. You can turn them into a multi-colored flotilla by using peppers in as many hues — green, red, yellow, white, chocolate brown — as you can find.

¼ lb/120 g riso or orzo, cooked (see page 10)

▪

4 medium bell peppers (capsicums), in mixed colors

6 to 8 cloves garlic (or to taste), finely chopped

2 tablespoons/30 g/1 oz butter

5 tablespoons olive oil, divided

1 can (2 oz/60 g) anchovy fillets, drained and finely chopped

½ cup/120 mL/4 fl oz dry white wine

1 tablespoon lemon juice

½ cup/90 g/3 oz roasted red bell pepper (capsicum), see page 140, finely chopped

2 tablespoons capers

¼ cup/30 g/1 oz fresh parsley leaves, finely chopped

Salt and freshly ground black pepper to taste

Halve peppers lengthwise; remove stems, seeds and membranes. Blanch 5 minutes in boiling water; drain.

Sauté garlic in butter and 1 tablespoon olive oil over medium heat, stirring frequently, until it turns fragrant and golden but does not burn, about 3 to 5 minutes. Mash in anchovies; add wine and lemon juice and cook until slightly reduced. Remove from heat and stir in roasted red peppers, capers, parsley and cooked riso. Adjust seasonings.

Fill peppers with pasta mixture and arrange in an ovenproof pan. Drizzle remaining olive oil over peppers. Cover pan and bake 30 minutes in a preheated oven (350°/180°C/gas mark 4). Serve hot or warm.

To Drink: Any lively, refreshing white or sparkling wine — nothing too heavy — will complement the rich, salty flavors of the sea in this dish.

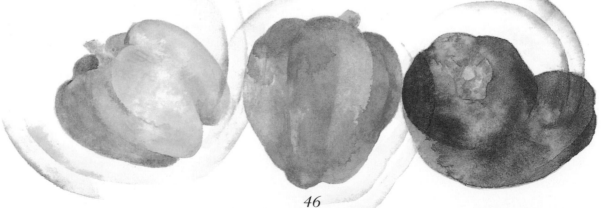

SOUPS

Everyone loves soup. It's soothing, warming, nourishing; the ultimate comfort food for those dark days of winter. And in the summertime, it's the perfect meal in a bowl for those long, lazy evenings when you crave a quick, simple supper. Rustic or refined, it's forever versatile and variable — whether you start an elegant dinner with a cup of suave bisque, greet friends with a mug of chunky chowder or sit down with family to a homey seafood stew.

Juicy noodles and plump nuggets of fish and shellfish bubbling in the stockpot have universal appeal — every part of the world enjoys a wealth of local specialties. You can just about cook your way around the globe with the recipes here, from a fragrant French Bouillabaisse to a silken Egg Flower Soup from China; from the sumptuous spice of Moroccan Shellfish Couscous to the five-alarm flames of Louisiana's Seafood Jambalaya.

Your soups, stews and chowders can be as time-honored or as new-spirited as you choose. As our grandmothers discovered before us, a simmering kettle inspires a cook's creative flair with flavors, colors and textures. The recipes here give you a wide range of options. Some highlight the seafood, with noodles adding substance and carrying the broth's rich essence. Others feature the noodles, with the seafood contributing its subtle, elusive flavors. Still others balance fish and pasta in a partnership of equals. And whether your potage's palette is ablaze with color, as it is in the brilliant red Nordic Winter Soup, or quietly understated, as in Spicy Pasta Fazool', these soups, stews and chowders will delight your eye as well as your palate.

Cook up a big batch of seafood noodle soup, then, in any of its infinite varieties — and serve it either straight from the pot or from your prettiest tureen. You'll bring a world of enjoyment to family and friends.

My Mom's Baked Burrida

The following trio of recipes — robust stewy soups spooned with garlicky sauce — share a proud Mediterranean heritage. The first is based on a favorite of my mom's, a specialty of the Italian Riviera. It's a great party dish, so why not make a big batch like this, which serves about a dozen.

1 lb/500 g gemelli, cooked al dente (see page 10)
¼ cup/60 mL/2 fl oz olive oil
Salt to taste

·

2 large onions, finely chopped
6 garlic cloves, finely minced
2 tablespoons fresh oregano or marjoram leaves
4 anchovy fillets, drained and finely chopped or mashed
2 lb/1 kg monkfish, sole, butterfish or other mild white fish fillets, cut into thumb-length pieces (include several varieties if possible)
1 lb/500 g prawns, peeled and deveined
3 dozen medium mussels
1 dozen cherrystone or other juicy clams
4 small lobster tails, cracked, or 1 lb/500 g crab in the shell, cleaned and cracked
3 cups/750 g/1½ lb coarsely chopped fresh or canned tomatoes
1 cup/250 mL/8 fl oz dry white wine
¼ cup/60 mL/2 fl oz olive oil
Salt and freshly ground pepper to taste

Basil Aioli
2 cups/500 mL/16 fl oz mayonnaise, preferably homemade (see page 139)
4 to 6 cloves garlic, or to taste, finely minced or squeezed through a garlic press
2 cups/250 g/8 oz fresh basil leaves

Place cooked pasta in a large baking dish and toss with olive oil and salt. Combine onions, garlic, oregano and anchovies. Layer half the onion mixture over pasta, then the fish fillets and prawns, the remaining onion mixture and the mussels, clams and lobster or crab. Top with tomatoes, wine and olive oil. Season to taste.

Cover and bake in a preheated 375°F/190°C/gas mark 5 oven for 45 minutes to 1 hour. Serve hot with Basil Aioli on the side.

For Basil Aioli: Blend basil and garlic into mayonnaise (if making your own mayonnaise, add these ingredients to the egg mixture before blending in the oil) and process until basil is finely chopped. Pass separately.

To Drink: With this supremely versatile dish, Mom always served both white and red Italian wine for guests to help themselves. So do I, and so can you — just be sure the whites aren't too sweet or the reds too heavy.

Easy Bouillabaisse with Angelhair

Every town along the French Riviera has its own version of bouillabaisse, the classic regional seafood soup-stew. My translation substitutes a tangle of angelhair pasta for the traditional crust of bread. Do as the French do and make use of the freshest fish you can find — in as many varieties as possible.

∙

½ lb/250 g angelhair

Soup Base
4 cloves garlic, finely minced
¼ lb/120 g shallots, finely minced
¼ cup/60 mL/2 fl oz olive oil
1 medium carrot, thinly sliced
2 stalks fresh fennel or celery, diced
5 cups/1.25 L/40 fl oz Fish Stock (see page 139)
2 tablespoons Pernod or other anise-flavored liquor
2 tablespoons finely minced or grated orange zest
¼ teaspoon saffron
Salt and freshly ground black pepper to taste

∙

1 lb/500 g medium prawns, peeled and deveined
½ lb/250 g monkfish, cut into pieces (2 in/5 cm)
1 lb/500 g sea bass or cod, cut into pieces (2 in/5 cm)
½ lb/250 g small scallops

Rouille
4 to 6 cloves garlic, or to taste, finely minced
1 tablespoon ground paprika
¼ to ½ teaspoon cayenne, or to taste
2 cups mayonnaise/500 mL/16 fl oz, preferably homemade (see page 139)

Sauté garlic and shallots in olive oil over low-medium heat, stirring often, until they are soft and fragrant, about 5 to 7 minutes. Stir in carrots and fennel and cook, covered, 1 to 2 minutes. Add stock, Pernod, orange zest and saffron and simmer 15 to 20 minutes. Add seafood and simmer until just cooked through, 2 to 3 minutes. Adjust seasonings.

For Rouille: While broth is simmering, blend garlic, paprika and cayenne into mayonnaise (if making your own mayonnaise, add these ingredients to the egg mixture before blending in the oil).

Also while broth is simmering cook angelhair (see page 10) about 5 minutes. Transfer seafood to a warmed serving bowl. Add angelhair and heat through. Ladle into individual soup bowls, twirling pasta into "nests." Serve hot with Rouille on the side and let diners help themselves to the assorted seafood.

To Drink: For easygoing, self-service entertaining, offer an assortment of dry white wines — from France or California or both — plus a good-quality dry rosé or light red, and let everyone help themselves.

Provençal-Style Fisherman's Stew

This version of the Provençal classic, soupe au pistou, brims with fresh vegetables and a netful of assorted seafood. Its accompaniment, a garlicky, basil-laced pistou, like the Italian pesto, is traditionally made with a mortar and pestle. This hearty recipe serves about 8.

½ lb/250 g creste di gallo or other medium textured pasta

∎

1 lb/500 g medium mussels
1 lb/500 g medium clams
1 cup/250 mL/8 fl oz dry white wine

Stew Base

2 medium onions, finely chopped
¼ cup/60 mL/2 fl oz olive oil
8 cloves garlic, finely minced
2 medium leeks, white part only, thinly sliced
1 medium red bell pepper (capsicum), thinly sliced
2 medium zucchini (courgettes), thinly sliced
4 cups/1 kg/2 lb finely chopped fresh or canned tomatoes
3 cups/750 mL/24 fl oz Fish Stock (see page 139)

∎

lb/250 g string (French green) beans, halved and cooked crisp-tender
1 lb/500 g sea bass or cod, cut into strips (½ in/1 cm)
1 lb/500 g squid (calamari), cleaned and cut into rings (½ in/1 cm)
1 lb/500 g medium prawns, peeled and deveined
¼ cup/30 g/1 oz fresh parsley leaves, coarsely chopped
¼ cup/30 g/1 oz fresh basil leaves, coarsely chopped
Salt and freshly ground black pepper to taste

Pistou

2 cups/250 g/8 oz fresh basil leaves
½ cup/120 mL/4 fl oz olive oil
3 to 6 cloves garlic, or to taste
2 tablespoons pine nuts (kernels)
½ (2 oz/60 g) can anchovy fillets, drained and finely chopped
2 tablespoons tomato paste (purée), optional

Steam mussels and clams with wine until they open, about 5 minutes. Strain and reserve liquid.

Sauté onions in olive oil over medium heat until soft and translucent, about 5 to 7 minutes. When onions are almost done, stir in garlic and sauté until soft and fragrant. Stir in leeks, bell pepper and zucchini and cook, covered, 2 to 3 minutes. Add tomatoes, Fish Stock and reserved clam and mussel liquid. Simmer 15 to 20 minutes. Meanwhile, cook pasta (see page 10) about 12 minutes. Add string beans and pasta to broth and heat through. Stir in bass or cod, squid, prawns, parsley and basil; simmer until seafood is barely cooked through, about 1 to 2 minutes. Adjust seasonings and serve hot with Pistou on the side.

For Pistou: Purée all ingredients in a blender (liquidizer) or food processor until smooth. (The optional tomato paste adds a delicious flavor, but at the loss of the bright green basil color.) Scrape into a small serving bowl and allow guests to spoon over individual portions.

To Drink: Robust fare in party quantities calls for uncomplicated wines, either red or white, poured freely from carafes. Just keep the wine dry and not too overpowering, and the glassware simple.

Mussel-Leek Bisque

*This very simple, clean-flavored soup makes a lovely light first course when your main dish
is rich and filling. If you like a touch of heat, the chiles spice it nicely.*

⅜ lb/185 g acini di pepe or other tiny pasta

·

3 dozen medium mussels
½ cup/120 mL/4 fl oz white wine
2 to 3 cups/500 to 750 mL/16 to 24 fl oz Fish Stock (see page 139)
2 large leeks, split, washed and thinly sliced (white part only)
¼ cup/60 mL/2 fl oz olive oil
4 to 6 cloves garlic, finely minced
1 to 2 small fresh hot red chiles, finely minced, optional
1 cup/250 mL/8 fl oz half-and-half (half milk, half cream)
¼ teaspoon saffron
¼ cup/30 g/1 oz fresh parsley leaves, coarsely chopped
Salt and freshly ground white or black pepper to taste

Steam mussels with wine until they open, about 5 minutes. Strain liquid, add
enough Fish Stock to equal 4 cups/1 L/32 fl oz total and set aside.

Sauté leeks in olive oil over medium heat until soft and translucent, about 7
to 10 minutes. When leeks are almost done, stir in garlic and chiles, if used, and
sauté until soft and fragrant.

Stir in reserved liquid. Add half-and-half and saffron and simmer 20
minutes.

About three-quarters through, cook the pasta (see page 10) about 5 minutes.
Add to broth with the parsley and mussels and heat through. Adjust seasonings
and serve hot.

To Drink: Without the chiles, a dry, crisp white wine works well; with them, a
touch of sweetness or fruitiness in the wine makes a better match.

Egg Flower Soup with Salmon

This is an elegant yet easy version of the ubiquitous egg flower, or egg drop soup, a mainstay of Chinese restaurants. The soup's residual heat cooks the beaten eggs and the gentle circular stirring motion spins them into long, delicate strands.

2 oz/60 g wonton wrappers,** cut into strips (¼ in/.5 cm), cooked (see page 13)

·

2 tablespoons cornstarch (cornflour powder)
½ tablespoon soy sauce
1 tablespoon sesame oil**
1 tablespoon fresh ginger juice (see page 140)
5 cups/1.25 L/40 fl oz Fish Stock (see page 139)
¾ lb/375 g salmon fillet, cut into strips (2 in/5 cm)
1 cup/185 g/6 oz fresh or frozen peas
2 green onions, thinly sliced (white plus 2 in/5 cm green)
Salt to taste
2 eggs, lightly beaten

Stir cornstarch with soy sauce, sesame oil and ginger juice until smooth. Add to stock and simmer until thickened slightly, about 5 minutes. Add salmon and peas; simmer until barely cooked through, 2 to 3 minutes. Stir in green onion and wonton strips and adjust seasonings. Turn off heat and stir eggs into soup, using a gentle circular motion. Serve hot.

To Drink: A beer or a light, fruity white wine will do nicely — and if you're feeling festive, uncork a salmon-colored blanc de noirs sparkling wine to match the color of the salmon in the soup.

Hot and Sour Seafood Soup

There seem to be just about as many variations of this staple Chinese soup as there are cooks who prepare it. This simple version, with shrimp, crab and tofu, packs a lot of protein — and adding the rice-like riso or orzo pasta makes it even more substantial.

¼ lb/120 g riso or orzo

Stock
2 tablespoons cornstarch (cornflour powder)
2 tablespoons water
5 cups/1.25 L/40 fl oz Fish Stock (see page 139)
¼ lb/120 g fresh shiitake mushrooms,** trimmed and thinly sliced
1 cup/120 g/4 oz canned straw mushrooms,** drained
⅓ cup/80 mL/3 fl oz rice vinegar
¼ cup/20 g/¾ oz grated carrot
½ to 1 teaspoon freshly ground black pepper, or to taste
½ to 1 teaspoon freshly ground white pepper, or to taste
1 tablespoon fresh ginger juice (see page 140)
Salt to taste
∙
⅓ lb/155 g/5 oz cooked shrimp
⅓ lb/155 g/5 oz cooked crabmeat
½ cup/120 g/4 oz tofu,** any style, diced
2 green (spring) onions, thinly sliced (white plus 2 in/5 cm green)

Mix cornstarch with water to form a thin paste. Combine cornstarch with the remaining ingredients for stock and simmer 20 minutes. About halfway through, cook the riso (see page 10) about 8 minutes. Add it, the shrimp, crab, tofu and green onions to broth; heat through. Adjust seasonings and serve hot.

To Drink: Relax with a light-bodied beer or a simple, fruity white wine.

**Available in Asian groceries or some supermarkets.

Spicy Sizzling Noodle Soup

Add some sizzle to your next dinner party. Drop these richly seasoned noodle cakes into each bowl of fragrant broth and your guests will be as delighted by the dramatic sound effects as by the intriguing tastes.

Broth

**5 cups/1.25 L/40 fl oz Fish Stock (see page 139,
preferably made with shrimp shells)**
2 tablespoons dried shrimp**
½ cup/120 mL/4 fl oz Shaohsing rice wine** or dry sherry
¼ lb/120 g fresh shiitake mushrooms,** thinly sliced
4 to 6 cloves garlic, or to taste, finely minced or squeezed through a garlic press

Noodle Cakes

½ lb/250 g fresh Chinese-style noodles,** cooked (see page 10)
1 tablespoon sesame oil**
½ to 1 teaspoon chili oil,** or to taste (optional)
1 tablespoon hoisin sauce**
½ tablespoon dark soy sauce**
2 green (spring) onions, thinly sliced (white part plus 2 in/5 cm green)
¼ cup/60 mL/2 fl oz peanut or other vegetable oil

■

1 tablespoon fresh ginger juice (see page 140)
**½ cup/90 g/3 oz snow peas (mange tout), cut in diagonal strips (½ in/1 cm), or
½ cup/90 g/3 oz fresh or frozen peas**
½ to 1 small fresh hot red chile, or to taste, finely minced
2 green (spring) onions, thinly sliced (white plus 2 in/5 cm green)
½ lb/250 g cooked tiny shrimp

Simmer broth ingredients 20 minutes to blend flavors.

For Noodle Cakes: Drain noodles and toss with sesame oil, chili oil, hoisin sauce, dark soy sauce and green onions. Heat 1 scant tablespoon peanut oil in a small nonstick skillet over medium-high heat. Transfer about one-sixth of the noodles to skillet and press down flat; cook until crisp and golden brown, about 3 to 5 minutes. Turn and repeat for second side. Keep warm while you prepare a noodle cake for each serving. (You can speed up the process by using a larger skillet and making three noodle cakes at once.)

Just before serving, stir ginger juice, snow peas, chile pepper, green onions and cooked shrimp into soup and heat through. Ladle into individual bowls. Top each serving with a noodle cake and serve immediately.

Variation: Make one giant noodle pancake, place hot soup in a large bowl or tureen, add sizzling hot noodle cake and serve family style.

To Drink: A fruity, slightly sweet white, an off-dry sparkling wine, a light red, or a glass of warm Shaohsing rice wine are all pleasant partners.

**Available in Asian groceries or some supermarkets

Seafood Sukiyaki

Despite its many ingredients, this wholesome one-pot meal is quite easy to put together. A sea-food version of the Japanese winter staple, it can provide the centerpiece for a homey, relaxed evening with friends. Just keep the sukiyaki pot simmering at the table (a flame-proof or electric fondue pot is ideal) and let everyone help themselves.

1 package (7 oz/220 g) shirataki, packed in water, rinsed and drained**

Sukiyaki Broth
6 cups/1.5 L/48 fl oz Fish Stock (see page 139)
¼ cup/60 mL/2 fl oz soy sauce
½ cup/120 mL/4 fl oz sake**
2 tablespoons sugar
4 thin slices ginger
■
1 medium carrot, thinly sliced
2 cups/250 g/8 oz napa (Chinese) cabbage, thinly sliced
½ red (Spanish) onion, cut into wedges (½ in/1 cm)
4 green (spring) onions, cut into diagonal pieces (1 in/2.5 cm)
¼ lb/120 g/4 oz fresh shiitake mushrooms, thinly sliced**
½ lb/250 g/8 oz salmon fillet, cut into strips (½ in/1 cm)
**½ lb/250 g/8 oz rock cod or other firm-fleshed white fish,
cut into strips (½ in/1 cm)**
½ lb/250 g/8 oz scallops
½ lb/250 g/8 oz prawns, peeled and deveined
4 oz/120 g packaged fish cake (kamaboko), thinly sliced**
½ cup/60 g/2 oz canned straw mushrooms, drained**
1 cup/250 g/8 oz tofu, diced**

Combine ingredients for Broth and simmer 20 minutes. Remove ginger.

Stir in carrot, cabbage, red and green onions and shiitake mushrooms; simmer 3 minutes. Add salmon, cod, scallops and prawns and simmer until barely cooked through, 2 to 3 minutes. Stir in shirataki, fish cake, straw mushrooms and tofu and heat through. Transfer to fondue pot and serve hot.

To Drink: Go with the traditional sake or beer, or a medium-bodied white or sparkling wine with this full-flavored soup.

**Available in Asian groceries or some supermarkets

Thai Fish Soup

Exotic, tantalizing and complex, the flavors that lure you time and again to your favorite Thai restaurant are surprisingly easy to duplicate at home. The wriggly, see-through glass noodles, made from mung beans, add texture and a touch of whimsy.

6 oz/185 g glass noodles, soaked (see page 10)**

Stock
5 cups/1.25 L/40 fl oz Fish Stock (see page 139)
1 cup/120 g/4 oz unsweetened canned pineapple, cut into chunks (½ in/1 cm)
½ cup/120 mL/4 fl oz juice from canned pineapple
1 small fresh hot red chile, thinly sliced, or to taste
4 kaffir lime leaves or 1 length (6 in/15 cm) lemongrass** or 1 tablespoon
finely minced lime zest**
2 tablespoons lime juice
2 tablespoons Shaohsing rice wine or dry sherry**
1 tablespoon fresh ginger juice (see page 140)
2 garlic cloves, finely minced
•
1 dozen clams (about 1 lb/500 g)
1 dozen mussels (about 1 lb/500 g)
½ cup/120 mL/4 fl oz water
1 lb/500 g rock cod, cut into chunks (1 in/2.5 cm)
1 cup/250 mL/8 fl oz canned coconut milk**
Salt to taste
•
¼ cup/30 g/1 oz fresh cilantro (coriander) leaves, coarsely chopped
2 green (spring) onions, thinly sliced (white plus 2 in/5 cm green)

Drain noodles and cut into lengths (4 in/10 cm).

Combine all the ingredients for stock and simmer 20 minutes. While the stock is simmering, steam clams and mussels with water until they open, about 5 minutes. Strain liquid and add to stock. Remove lemongrass if used. Add rock cod and simmer until barely done (fish should flake easily), 2 to 3 minutes. Stir in noodles, coconut milk, clams and mussels and heat through. Adjust seasonings. Garnish with cilantro and green onions and serve hot.

To Drink: In a Thai restaurant you'd probably order a beer or a sweet, milky Thai iced tea with this. A light, fruity or slightly sweet white or sparkling wine would certainly be an option.

**Available in Asian groceries or some supermarkets

Curried Salmon and Scallops

This soupy Thai-style curry is as easy to make as it is delicious. Instead of the usual bed of rice, the angelhair nests set off the colors of salmon, scallops and peas beautifully.

½ lb/250 g angelhair nests

Curry Sauce
1 medium onion, thinly sliced
2 cloves garlic, finely minced
2 tablespoons peanut or other vegetable oil
1½ cups/375 mL/12 fl oz Fish Stock (see page 139)
1 cup/250 mL/8 fl oz canned coconut milk**
2 tablespoons lime juice
1 to 2 tablespoons green curry paste,** or to taste
½ lb/250 g salmon fillets, cut into 2 in/5 cm strips
½ lb/250 g medium scallops
½ lb/250 g snow peas (mange tout), cooked crisp-tender
2 green (spring) onions, thinly sliced (white plus 2 in/5 cm green)
Salt and freshly ground pepper to taste

Sauté onion and garlic in oil over low-medium heat, stirring often, until soft and fragrant, about 5 to 7 minutes. Add Fish Stock, coconut milk, lime juice and curry paste and simmer 10 minutes.

About halfway through, cook the angelhair (see page 10) about 5 minutes.

Meanwhile, add salmon, scallops, snow peas and green onions to the broth and simmer until fish is just cooked through, 2 to 3 minutes. Adjust seasonings.

Arrange angelhair nests in a deep serving platter or individual soup bowls. Divide seafood and sauce over pasta, filling the nests, and serve hot.

To Drink: If you're not having Thai iced tea or beer, a fruity or slightly sweet white or sparkling wine does nicely.

**Available in Asian groceries or some supermarkets

Miso Soup with Ramen and Tempura

Crisply fried, lacy tempura, one of the best-loved of Japanese foods, is actually a legacy of six-teenth-century Portuguese seamen and missionaries. Its modern version includes seafood and vegetables of all sorts. Served on a tangle of springy ramen noodles in a protein-laden miso broth, the tempura tidbits complete a nourishing, well-rounded meal.

½ lb/250 g fresh ramen noodles**

Miso Soup
4 cups/1 L/32 fl oz Fish Stock (see page 139)
1 cup/250 mL/8 fl oz sake**
½ cup/155 g/5 oz yellow (shinshu) or white (shiro) miso**
2 green (spring) onions, thinly sliced (white plus 2 in/5 cm green)

Tempura Batter
1 cup/155 g/5 oz all-purpose (plain) flour
2 teaspoons baking powder
1 egg plus one egg yolk
1 teaspoon salt
2 cups/500 mL/16 fl oz cold water

Dipping Sauce
1 cup/250 mL/8 fl oz Fish Stock (see page 139)
½ cup/45 g/1½ oz grated daikon** (Japanese radish)
¼ cup/60 mL/2 fl oz soy sauce
2 tablespoons lemon juice
1 tablespoon fresh ginger juice (see page 140)
4 cups/1 L/32 fl oz peanut or other vegetable oil

▪

1 lb/500 g medium shrimp or prawns, peeled and deveined
½ lb/250 g asparagus tips, broccoli florets, string (French green) beans, or a combination
1 bunch green (spring) onions (white plus 2 in/5 cm green)
1 medium yam or sweet potato, halved lengthwise
and cut into long sticks (½ in x ½ in/1 cm x 1 cm)
6 large fresh shiitake** or regular mushrooms, or a combination, halved

For Miso Soup: Simmer Fish Stock and sake 15 to 20 minutes to evaporate alcohol and blend flavors. Stir in miso and green onions and heat through.

For Tempura Batter: Immediately before cooking, whisk ingredients together quickly with a fork. For best results, the batter should be cold, thin, and a little bit lumpy.

For Dipping Sauce: Combine all ingredients and divide equally among small individual bowls.

For tempura: Heat oil to 375°F/190°C. Dip prawns and vegetables in batter and fry in oil, a few at a time, until crisp and golden. Remove with a slotted spoon and drain on a rack or paper towels.

While tempura is frying, cook ramen about 2 minutes and divide among individual bowls. Spoon hot Miso Soup over ramen and top with tempura. Serve hot, with dipping sauce on the side.

To Drink: Warmed sake or cold beer would be traditional here; you can also try an off-dry white or sparkling wine.

**Available in Asian groceries or some supermarkets

Greek Shellfish Stew

*In many Mediterranean dishes, the licoricey tones of anise and fennel are used to accent the
natural sweetness of shellfish. This light yet satisfying Greek stew uses this flavor in three forms
– the crisp fresh bulb, the crunchy seeds and the potent liquor.*

⅜ lb/185 g orzo or riso

▪

1 lb/500 g small clams
1 lb/500 g medium mussels
1 cup/250 mL/8 fl oz dry white wine

▪

1 medium onion, finely chopped
2 tablespoons olive oil
2 tablespoons/30 g/1 oz butter
2 cloves garlic, finely minced
3 stalks fresh fennel (anise), thinly sliced
1 tablespoon ouzo or anisette
1 teaspoon anise or fennel seeds
1 lb/500 g medium prawns, peeled and deveined
1 lb/500 g squid (calamari), cleaned and cut into pieces (1 in/2.5 cm)
3 cups/250 ml/24 fl oz Fish Stock (see page 139), warmed
2 tablespoons lemon juice
½ cup/60 g/2 oz fresh parsley leaves, coarsely chopped, plus extra for garnish
Salt and freshly ground white or black pepper to taste

Steam clams and mussels with wine until they open, about 5 minutes. Strain
and reserve liquid.

Cook orzo (see page 10) about 8 minutes.

Meanwhile, sauté onion in olive oil and butter over medium heat until soft
and translucent, about 5 to 7 minutes. When onions are almost done, stir in
garlic and sauté until soft and fragrant. Add fresh fennel, ouzo and anise or
fennel seeds; stir 1 minute to wilt fennel slightly. Stir in prawns and squid and
cook, stirring, until they just start to change color, about 1 to 2 minutes. Add
Fish Stock, reserved clam and mussel liquid and lemon juice. Simmer until
prawns and squid are barely cooked through, about 2 to 3 minutes.

Add clams, mussels, parsley and orzo and heat through. Adjust seasonings
and serve hot.

To Drink: With this delicate soup, you'll probably do best with a dry or slightly
sweet medium-weight white or sparkling wine.

Moroccan Shellfish Couscous

*Couscous, a staple of Moroccan cuisine, is a very fine-grained semolina pasta.
Traditionally steamed for hours in a special kettle and served with a savory stew of fish,
poultry, vegetables or meat, it makes a varied and versatile meal in a bowl. This easy
seafood version, which calls for quick-cooking instant couscous (and an authentic dab of
flamethrowing harissa paste), makes enough to feed a hungry horde of 10 or so.*

⅝ lb/315 g instant couscous**

∎

3 dozen medium mussels (about 2 lbs/1 kg)
3 dozen small littleneck or Manila clams (about 2lbs/1 kg)
1 cup/250 mL/8 fl oz dry white wine or water
2 to 3 cups/500 to 750 mL/16 to 24 fl oz Fish Stock (see page 139) or clam juice
(see below)

∎

2 medium onions, coarsely chopped
¼ cup/60 mL/2 fl oz olive oil
4 cloves garlic, finely minced
1 medium carrot, thinly sliced
2 medium zucchini (courgettes), diced
2 cups/500 g/1 lb finely chopped fresh or canned tomatoes
¼ cup/60 mL/2 fl oz lemon juice
½ cup/185 g/6 oz chopped dates or raisins
¼ cup/30 g/1 oz slivered almonds
½ tablespoon ground cumin
2 (3 in/2.5 cm) cinnamon sticks
1 lb/500 g rock cod, cut into cubes (1 in/2.5 cm)
Salt and freshly ground pepper to taste
½ to 1 tablespoon harissa** (Moroccan hot pepper paste) or cayenne to taste

Steam mussels and clams with wine or water until shells open, about 5 minutes.
Strain liquid, add enough Fish Stock to equal 4 cups (1 L/32 fl oz) and set aside.

Sauté onions in olive oil over medium heat until soft and translucent, about 5
to 7 minutes. When onions are almost done, stir in garlic and sauté until soft
and fragrant. Stir in carrot, zucchini and tomatoes and cook until slightly softened, 5 to 7 minutes. Add reserved liquid, lemon juice, dates, almonds, cumin
and cinnamon and simmer 5 to 7 minutes, until vegetables are crisp-tender. Stir
in rock cod and simmer until just cooked through, about 2 minutes. Add clams
and mussels, heat thoroughly, adjust seasonings and add harissa to taste.

Prepare couscous according to package directions. (Or place in a bowl, add
3 cups/750 mL/24 fl oz salted boiling water and cover for 5 minutes.) Fluff
with a fork.

To serve, mound couscous in a deep serving platter or divide among individual
bowls. Ladle broth, vegetables and seafood over couscous and serve hot.

To Drink: Sweetness and spice in food call for a sweet beverage — a refreshing
white or sparkling wine or even a light, fruity red.

**Available in Middle Eastern groceries and some supermarkets

Tunisian Mussel Soup

This rather exotic dish balances the sweet, comforting flavor of cinnamon with the piquant spice of cumin and the heat of cayenne. You can vary the proportions to suit your own taste.

¼ lb/120 g filini, or 1-inch/2.5 cm pieces vermicelli
•
3 dozen medium mussels (about 2 lbs/1 kg)
½ cup/120 mL/4 fl oz water
•
1 medium onion, finely chopped
¼ cup/60 mL/2 fl oz olive oil
2 leeks, white part only, thinly sliced
2 stalks celery, with leaves, thinly sliced
3 cups/750 g/1½ lb finely chopped fresh or canned tomatoes
2 cups/500 mL/16 fl oz Fish Stock (see page 139)
2 tablespoons lemon juice
1 teaspoon ground cumin
1 teaspoon ground cinnamon
½ teaspoon cayenne, or to taste
1 cup/120 g/4 oz fresh parsley leaves, coarsely chopped
2 green (spring) onions, thinly sliced (white plus 2 in/5 cm green)
Salt and freshly ground pepper to taste

Steam mussels with water until they open, about 5 minutes. Strain and reserve liquid. Sauté onion in olive oil over medium heat until soft and translucent, about 5 to 7 minutes. Stir in leeks and celery; sauté until slightly wilted, about 4 to 5 minutes. Add reserved mussel liquid, tomatoes, Fish Stock, lemon juice, cumin, cinnamon and cayenne. Simmer 20 minutes to blend flavors.

About three-quarters through, cook the filini (see page 10). Stir into broth with parsley, green onions and mussels; heat through. Adjust seasonings and serve hot.

To Drink: This spicy, tomato-rich dish can handle a light- to medium-bodied fruity red wine, as well as slightly sweet whites and sparklers.

*Spicy Pasta Fazool'

Hot, spicy and nourishing, with the smooth and comforting texture of long-simmered white kidney beans, this hearty minestra is a winter delight. (Use canned beans and it's an extra-quick one, too.) Pasta fazool', Neapolitan dialect for pasta e fagioli, simply means "pasta and beans." Delicious variations on this classic dish abound throughout Italy. They all taste even better the next day.

¼ lb/120 g ditalini, cooked (see page 10)

•

2 cans (15 oz/450 g each) cannellini beans** (white kidney beans), undrained
1 can (2 oz/60 g) anchovies, drained and finely chopped or mashed
3 cups/750 mL/24 fl oz vegetable stock or water
½ cup/90 g/3 oz finely chopped red (Spanish) onion
2 cloves garlic, finely minced
¼ cup/60 mL/2 fl oz extra-virgin olive oil
1 tablespoon lemon juice
¼ teaspoon dried hot red pepper flakes, or to taste
½ tablespoon freshly ground black pepper, or to taste
Salt to taste

•

¼ cup/30 g/1 oz parsley leaves, coarsely chopped
½ cup/90 g/3 oz grated parmesan cheese

If using dried beans, rinse and pick over; soak overnight in warm water. Rinse and drain beans; place in a flameproof, ovenproof pot; cover with water and bring to a boil. Cover tightly and bake in a preheated oven (350°F/180°C/gas mark 4) until tender, about 1 to 1¼ hours.

Combine all the ingredients in a medium-sized pot. Bring to a boil and simmer 3 to 5 minutes to blend flavors. Adjust seasonings and top with parsley and half the parmesan cheese. Serve hot, and pass the remaining parmesan.

To Drink: You can add to the warming effect of this soup with a rustic Italian red, a Zinfandel or Barbera or a good blended red table wine.

**Available in Italian groceries and some supermarkets

Pasta Paella with Riso

In a traditional Spanish paella, which usually contains some combination of meat, sausage, chicken, and even snails as well as seafood, raw rice simmers slowly in a saffron-flecked stew base. This easy, colorful, all-seafood adaptation — enough to feed a dozen or more — streamlines the original by substituting rice-shaped riso pasta, cooking completely on the stovetop.

1½ lb/750 g riso or orzo

∙

2 dozen small clams (about 1½ lbs/750 g)
2 dozen medium mussels (about 1½ lbs/750 g)
1 cup/250 mL/8 fl oz dry white wine

∙

2 medium onions, finely chopped
2 tablespoons olive oil
2 tablespoons/30 g/1 oz butter
6 to 8 cloves garlic, finely minced
1 medium red bell pepper (capsicum), cut into thin strips
1 medium yellow bell pepper (capsicum), cut into thin strips
1 to 2 small fresh hot red chiles, finely minced
2 cups/500 g/1 lb finely chopped fresh or canned tomatoes
1 lb/500 g squid (calamari), cleaned and cut into rings
1 lb/500 g prawns, shelled and deveined
1 cup/185 g/6 oz fresh or frozen peas
⅓ cup/60 g/2 oz golden raisins (sultanas)
Generous pinch saffron
2 tablespoons fresh oregano or marjoram
1 teaspoon ground coriander
1 tablespoon finely minced or grated orange zest
1 to 2 cups/250 to 500 mL/8 to 16 fl oz Fish Stock (see page 139)
or clam broth, warmed
Salt and freshly ground white or black pepper, to taste

In a covered pot, steam clams and mussels with white wine until shells open, about 5 minutes. Strain and reserve broth.

In a paella pan or wide skillet, sauté onions in olive oil and butter over medium heat until soft and translucent, about 5 to 7 minutes.

Meanwhile, cook riso (see page 10) about 8 minutes.

When onions are almost done, stir in garlic and sauté until soft and fragrant. Stir in bell peppers, chiles and tomatoes; cook 2 to 3 minutes or until slightly softened. Stir in squid and prawns and cook until color just starts to change, about 1 to 2 minutes. Add peas, raisins, saffron, oregano, coriander, orange zest and reserved broth from mussels and clams. Simmer 2 minutes to blend flavors.

Stir in riso and heat through, adding enough fish stock or clam broth, if necessary, to make a slightly soupy texture. Stir in clams and mussels; adjust seasonings. Serve hot in paella pan or transfer to a soup tureen or serving bowl, arranging some of the seafood attractively on top.

To Drink: A refreshing off-dry white, sparkler or fruity red would do nicely — or mix up a punchbowl of sangria for an instant fiesta!

Nordic Winter Soup

Russia has its nourishing, comforting borscht; the chilly Scandinavian countries, too, base many hearty soups on beets and other root vegetables. You can intensify the naturally sweet flavor of these cold-weather treasures by baking, rather than boiling them.

2 oz/60 g anellini, tubetti or other small, hollow pasta

•

1 lb/500 g beets, halved or quartered, skins on
3 medium red (Spanish) onions, halved, skins on
2 heads garlic, halved horizontally
2 tablespoons olive oil
3 cups/750 mL/24 fl oz Fish Stock (see page 139) or vegetable stock
¼ cup/60 mL/2 fl oz lemon juice
Salt and freshly ground white or black pepper to taste

•

½ cup/120 mL/4 fl oz sour cream (crème fraîche)
½ lemon, thinly sliced, slices halved
1 bunch fresh chives, thinly sliced
Small dill sprigs
¼ lb/120 g smoked trout, whitefish, sable or other white fish, boned and cut into thin slivers

Wrap beets in foil; coat cut surfaces of onions and garlic with olive oil and wrap separately in foil. Bake in preheated oven (375°F/190°C/gas mark 4) until the onions and garlic are very soft and beets are firm-tender (45 minutes to 1½ hours, depending on type and size of vegetable). Slip off beet and onion skins; squeeze out garlic pulp. Chop beets into dice (¼ in/.5 cm).

Cook anellini (see page 10) about 5 minutes. Meanwhile, in a blender (liquidizer) or food processor, puree garlic and onions with stock and lemon juice. Transfer to a pot, stir in beets and heat through. Adjust seasonings.

To serve: Stir pasta into soup and heat through. Divide among individual soup bowls. Top each serving with sour cream, lemon slices, chives, dill and smoked fish. Serve hot.

To Drink: Pour a crisp white or sparkling wine to go with this chunky soup.

*New England Clam Chowder

One of the most warming of winter comfort foods is a steaming bowl of thick, creamy clam chowder, New England style. Why not update the old tried-and-true recipe with a handful of ditalini pasta? You won't even miss the potatoes!

¼ lb/120 g ditalini

■

1 medium onion, finely chopped
4 tablespoons/60 g/2 oz butter
2 cans (6 oz/185 g) chopped clams (baby clams), including liquid
1 cup/250 mL/8 fl oz clam broth or Fish Stock (see page 139)
2 tablespoons dry or medium-dry sherry
1 teaspoon ground mace or nutmeg
4 cups/1 L/32 fl oz whole milk or half-and-half (half milk, half cream)
¼ cup/30 g/1 oz fresh parsley leaves, coarsely chopped
Salt and freshly ground black or white pepper to taste

Cook ditalini (see page 10) about 8 minutes. Meanwhile, sauté onion in butter over low-medium heat, stirring often, until soft and translucent, about 7 to 10 minutes. Add clams, clam broth, sherry and mace; bring to a boil and simmer 5 minutes. Stir in milk, parsley and ditalini; heat just to boiling. Adjust seasonings and serve hot.

To Drink: A small glass of room-temperature sherry, not too sweet, would echo the sherry in the chowder — while adding to the soup's warming effect.

Shellfish Chowder

If you like Manhattan clam chowder, you'll love this hearty, seafood-laden stew. It tastes even better the next day, as the pasta soaks up the rich broth. (And you'll have plenty of plan-aheads!) For a more traditional flavor, halve the olive oil and substitute 2 strips of bacon, finely chopped.

½ lb/250 g maruzzine

■

2 dozen small clams (about 1½ lbs/750 g)
2 dozen medium mussels (about 1½ lbs/750 g)
½ cup/120 mL/4 fl oz dry white wine

■

2 medium onions, finely chopped
¼ cup/60 mL/2 fl oz olive oil
4 cloves garlic, finely minced
1 medium bell pepper (capsicum), diced
1 medium carrot, thinly sliced
4 cups/1 L/32 fl oz Fish Stock (see page 139)
3 cups/750 g/1½ lb coarsely chopped fresh or canned tomatoes
2 bay leaves
2 tablespoons fresh thyme leaves
1 teaspoon freshly ground black pepper
2 dozen medium prawns (about 1 lb/500 g), peeled and deveined
1 lb/500 g squid (calamari), cleaned and cut into rings (½ in/1 cm)
2 cups/500 g/1 lb oysters and their liquor (freshly shucked or from a jar)
½ cup/60 g/2 oz fresh parsley leaves, coarsely chopped
Salt to taste

Steam clams and mussels with wine until they open, about 5 minutes. Strain and reserve liquid.

Sauté onions in oil over medium heat until soft and translucent, about 5 to 7 minutes. When onions are almost done, stir in garlic, bell pepper and carrot, and sauté until garlic is soft and fragrant. Add reserved liquid, Fish Stock, tomatoes, bay leaves, thyme and pepper. Simmer 30 minutes.

Halfway through, cook the maruzzine (see page 10) about 12 minutes.

Add prawns, squid and oysters to broth; simmer until barely cooked, 1 to 2 minutes. Stir in clams, mussels, pasta and parsley and heat through. Adjust seasonings and serve hot.

To Drink: The hearty flavors of tomato, peppers and herbs stand up to either a light- to medium-bodied red or a dry, crisp, full-flavored white. Your choice.

Linguine with Cioppino

On San Francisco's Fisherman's Wharf, the sweet local Dungeness crab stars in a hearty seafood stew called cioppino. Serve it up with linguine, instead of the sourdough bread local to San Francisco, for a pasta-lover's feast.

1 lb/500 g linguine

∎

2 dozen medium mussels (about 1½ lbs/750 g)
½ cup/120 mL/4 fl oz dry white wine
2 medium onions, finely chopped
¼ cup/60 mL/2 fl oz olive oil
4 to 6 cloves garlic, finely minced, or to taste
1 medium bell pepper (capsicum), diced
2 stalks fresh fennel (anise) or celery, thinly sliced
2 cups/500 g/1 lb finely chopped fresh or canned tomatoes
1 cup/250 mL/8 fl oz Fish Stock (see page 139)
1 cup/250 mL/8 fl oz dry red or white wine
2 bay leaves
2 tablespoons fresh oregano or marjoram leaves
½ to 1 teaspoon dried hot red pepper flakes, or to taste
½ lb/250 g medium prawns, shelled and deveined
1 medium Dungeness crab (about 1½ lbs/750 g), cooked, cleaned and cracked
(see page 14; or equal amount of other type of crab in the shell)
½ cup/60 g/2 oz fresh parsley leaves, coarsely chopped
Salt and freshly ground black pepper to taste

Steam mussels with wine until open, about 5 minutes. Strain; reserve liquid.

Sauté onions in olive oil over medium heat until soft and translucent, about 5 to 7 minutes. When onions are almost done, stir in garlic, bell pepper and fennel and sauté until garlic is soft and fragrant.

Stir in tomatoes, stock, wine, reserved mussel liquid, bay leaves, oregano and hot pepper; simmer 20 minutes.

Halfway through, cook the linguine (see page 10) about 10 minutes.

Meanwhile, add prawns to sauce and simmer until just cooked through, about 1 to 2 minutes. Stir in crab, mussels and parsley and heat through. Adjust seasonings.

Toss linguine with about three-quarters of the sauce; top with seafood and remaining sauce. Serve hot.

To Drink: Cioppino lovers on Fisherman's Wharf favor simple red blends by the carafe — if you prefer white, a tart, herbal Sauvignon Blanc would be great.

Seafood Jambalaya on Riso

Since the word "jambalaya" has been traced to a combination of French, African and Cajun (Acadian) words, it seems apt that it sounds like "jumble." In the Louisiana bayous, a jambalaya is a colorful, flavorful and spicy potpourri featuring whatever the family hunter or fisherman manages to bag or net that day. My version replaces rice with riso.

½ lb/250 g riso or orzo

■

2 medium onions, finely chopped
4 tablespoons/60 g/2 oz butter
4 to 6 cloves garlic, finely minced
2 stalks celery, thinly sliced
½ medium red bell pepper (capsicum), diced
½ medium green bell pepper (capsicum), diced
2 cups/500 mL/16 fl oz puréed tomatoes
2 cups/500 mL/16 fl oz Fish Stock (see page 139)
2 bay leaves
½ tablespoon dried oregano
½ tablespoon dried thyme
½ to 1 tablespoon freshly ground white or black pepper, or to taste
½ to 1 teaspoon cayenne, or to taste
Salt to taste
1 lb shrimp, peeled and deveined
1 jar (10 oz/300 g) oysters, liquor included
1 lb/500 g cooked crab pieces in the shell, cleaned and cracked (see page 14)
1 lb/500 g rockfish fillet, cut into slices (1 in/2.5 cm)
½ cup/30 g/1 oz green (spring) onions, thinly sliced (white plus
2 in/5 cm green)

Sauté onions in butter over medium heat until soft and translucent, about 5 to 7 minutes. When onions are almost done, stir in garlic, celery and bell peppers and sauté until garlic is soft and fragrant. Add all remaining ingredients except seafood and green onions and simmer 15 minutes.

Halfway through, cook the riso (see page 10) about 8 minutes.

Meanwhile, stir seafood and green onions into sauce and simmer until seafood is just cooked through, about 2 to 3 minutes. Adjust seasonings and remove bay leaves.

Mound cooked riso in a wide serving bowl or divide among individual dishes. Spoon jambalaya around riso and serve hot.

To Drink: The hotter you spice this, the more you'll need a chilled mug of beer to fight the fire. If you take it easy on the cayenne, choose a fruity or slightly sweet white wine, or even a fruity red such as a Beaujolais or light Zinfandel.

Salmon-Sole Chowder

Here's a colorful, delicately flavored soup that can serve as a lovely light meal in itself or as a lead-in to a multi-course feast.

½ lb/250 g gemellini

∎

¼ lb/120 g shallots, finely minced
2 tablespoons/30 g/1 oz butter
1 medium carrot, thinly sliced
4 large stalks red chard (Swiss chard/silverbeet), cut into strips (¼ in/.5 cm)
4 cups/1 L/32 fl oz Fish Stock (see page 139)
1 cup/250 mL/8 fl oz half-and-half (half milk, half cream)
2 cups/375 g/12 oz fresh or frozen corn kernels
¼ cup/30 g/1 oz fresh parsley leaves, coarsely chopped
2 tablespoons paprika
½ lb/250 g salmon fillet, cut into 2 in/5 cm strips
¾ lb/375 g sole or flounder fillet, cut into 2 in/5 cm strips
Salt and freshly ground white or black pepper to taste

Sauté shallots in butter over low-medium heat, stirring often, until soft and fragrant, about 5 to 7 minutes. Stir in carrot, chard, stock and half-and-half and simmer 15 to 20 minutes.

Halfway through, cook the gemellini (see page 10) about 12 minutes.

Meanwhile, add corn, parsley, paprika, salmon and sole to broth and simmer until fish is just cooked through, about 2 to 3 minutes. Add pasta and heat through. Adjust seasonings and serve hot.

To Drink: You won't go wrong with a dry, medium-weight white wine, especially a medium-bodied Chardonnay or Sauvignon Blanc.

SALADS

Once upon a time, not very long ago, a salad was merely an afterthought — a throwaway course, almost, that refreshed your palate after the entree and set up your taste buds for dessert. It was green; it was cold. And it was, alas, downright boring.

Not anymore! In these times of health and fitness-consciousness, when eating light borders on a way of a life, salads have come out of the shadows and into the spotlight. Today as never before, salads show off a cook's true ingenuity with fresh, stylish ingredients. Nowadays, a salad can fill the bill either before or after the entree; as one of several equal courses, served in any order; or as a satisfying main dish in its own right.

The salads here are packed with color, texture and taste. They take full advantage of just-picked seasonal produce from garden and greengrocer. They'll keep you cool when the mercury climbs into the danger zone and bring a refreshing change of pace year-round. Both tasty and versatile, salads help you put a meal on the table without heating up the kitchen — or spending hours in it! But that's not all. No longer dull, or predictable — or even necessarily green, or cold — a well-crafted salad can open up a world of flavor possibilities. And what better way to transform a plate of greens into an exciting taste treat than with a fast-cooking, flavorful fusion of seafood and pasta? Whether it's a simple Shrimp and Artichoke Farfalle Salad or exotic Rice Sticks with Butterfish and Tropical Fruit Relish, seafood and pasta take the whole notion of salad into new realms. The salads that follow reflect many moods and explore many cuisines from all around the world. From the classic Tuscan White Bean Salad to the inventive, orange-and-green-hued New Zealand Mussel Salad; from the mellow, Spanish-style Mussel and Rockfish Escabeche to the riotously colored and textured Caribbean Conch Salad; you'll find just the right recipe to round out that special dinner — or make a meal all by itself!

*Summer Salad

With some herbs and cherry tomatoes, and a very few basics in your larder, you'll have all the makings for this late summer treat. Prepare it early in the day and slip it into the fridge to cool the pasta and blend the flavors.

1 lb/500 g vermicelli, cooked (see page 10)
¼ cup/60 mL/2 fl oz extra-virgin olive oil
Salt to taste
■
3 baskets (2 lb/1 kg) cherry tomatoes (mixed colors and varieties, if possible)
¼ cup/60 mL/2 fl oz extra-virgin olive oil
1 cup/120 g/4 oz fresh basil leaves, coarsely chopped
1 cup/120 g/4 oz fresh parsley leaves, coarsely chopped
4 to 6 cloves garlic, finely minced
2 cans (4 oz/120 g) oil-packed sardines, drained and mashed
½ teaspoon freshly ground black pepper, or to taste
¼ teaspoon dried hot red pepper flakes, or to taste
Salt to taste
Basil sprigs
Parsley sprigs

Toss vermicelli with olive oil and salt and chill.

Halve or quarter cherry tomatoes into bite-sized pieces. In a large bowl, mix them with olive oil, basil, parsley and garlic. Stir in sardines. Add black and red pepper; adjust seasonings. Toss pasta with about three-quarters of the sardine-tomato mixture and chill 1 to 2 hours. Top with the remaining sardine-tomato mixture, garnish with parsley and basil sprigs and serve chilled.

To Drink: A light, summery white wine such as a Soave, Valpolicella or good-quality table wine will enhance the easygoing mood of this refreshing dish.

*Spinach Salad with Whitefish

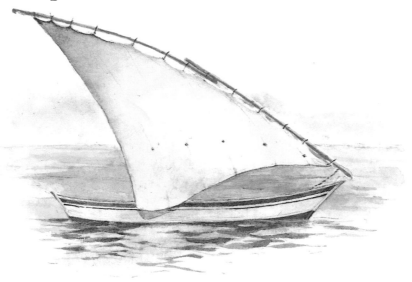

This cool, refreshing salad can perk up your appetite as a first course on a sultry summer evening or stand alone for Sunday brunch.

½ lb/250 g orecchiette or other small, textured pasta, cooked (see page 10)

Grapefruit-Pepper Dressing
½ cup/120 mL/4 fl oz tart grapefruit juice
2 tablespoons lemon juice
½ cup/120 mL/4 fl oz olive oil
½ teaspoon freshly ground white or black pepper
¼ cup/45 g/1½ oz finely chopped red (Spanish) onion
2 cloves garlic, finely minced
¼ cup/30 g/1 oz fresh parsley leaves, coarsely chopped
Salt to taste
▪
4 to 6 cups tender young spinach (English spinach) leaves
1 medium grapefruit, segmented
2 hard-boiled eggs, cut into wedges
2 cups/185 g/6 oz halved cherry tomatoes
6 to 8 oz/185 to 250 g smoked whitefish, boned and flaked

Combine all ingredients for Grapefruit-Pepper Dressing. Toss pasta with about three-quarters of the dressing; chill and arrange on spinach leaves. Arrange grapefruit sections, eggs, tomatoes and smoked fish on pasta and top with remaining dressing. Serve chilled.

To Drink: A fruity, off-dry white or sparkling wine, well chilled, matches nicely.

Mussel and Rockfish Escabeche

Invading Arabs brought the classic escabeche to Spain centuries before the refrigerator was invented. In it, the acidity of vinegar or lemon juice works to preserve cooked fish or poultry. Although this dish is traditionally served with bread, tiny pasta shells soak up the sauce just as well while their shape adds an echo of the sea.

½ lb/250 g maruzzine

∎

3 dozen mussels (about 2 lbs/1 kg)
½ cup/120 g/4 fl oz dry white wine
1 lb/500 g rock cod or other rockfish fillets
2 tablespoons all-purpose (plain) flour
¼ cup/60 mL/4 fl oz olive oil

∎

2 to 3 dozen small whole garlic cloves, peeled
¼ cup/60 mL/2 fl oz olive oil
2 medium onions, finely chopped
2 bay leaves
½ cup/120 mL/4 fl oz balsamic vinegar
¼ cup/60 mL/2 fl oz lemon juice
¼ cup/30 g/1 oz fresh parsley leaves, coarsely chopped
1 tablespoon fresh thyme leaves, coarsely chopped
1 tablespoon fresh oregano, coarsely chopped
1 tablespoon finely minced lemon zest
½ tablespoon ground paprika
½ teaspoon cayenne, or to taste (optional)
Salt and freshly ground pepper to taste

Steam mussels with wine until they open, about 5 minutes. Strain and reserve liquid. Dust rockfish with flour and sauté in olive oil over medium-high heat until just cooked, about 2 to 3 minutes per side. Chill mussels and rockfish.

Sauté garlic cloves in olive oil over very low heat until soft and golden, about 10 to 15 minutes. When garlic is almost done, stir in onions and bay leaves and sauté until onions are soft and translucent. Add remaining ingredients, including reserved mussel liquid. Heat through and adjust seasonings.

Pour sauce over mussels and rockfish and refrigerate at least 2 hours.

Cook maruzzine (see page 10) about 12 minutes.

Remove bay leaves from escabeche. Toss pasta with about three-quarters of the sauce; top with mussels, rockfish and remaining sauce. Serve chilled.

To Drink: There's enough depth of flavor in this dish to warrant a light red wine, or go with a crisp, dry white if you prefer.

*Spaghettini Niçoise

With tuna, anchovies, hard-boiled eggs and the best of the summer garden's bounty, the classic Salade Niçoise from the French Riviera makes a substantial yet refreshing summer meal. Instead of the usual new potatoes, I prefer a swirl of slim spaghettini to soak up the tangy dressing.

½ lb/250 g plain spaghettini, cooked (see page 10)
2 tablespoons extra-virgin olive oil
Salt to taste

Niçoise Dressing
½ cup/120 mL/4 fl oz extra-virgin olive oil
¼ cup/60 mL/2 fl oz red wine vinegar
2 tablespoons balsamic vinegar
1 teaspoon dry mustard
¼ cup/45 g/1½ oz finely minced red (Spanish) onion
¼ cup/30 g/1 oz fresh parsley leaves, coarsely chopped
¼ cup/30 g/1 oz fresh basil leaves, coarsely chopped
2 to 4 cloves garlic, finely minced
Salt and freshly ground pepper to taste

▪

1 can (6 oz/185 g) oil-packed tuna, preferably Italian,** flaked
2 hard-boiled eggs, cut into 6 wedges each
½ lb/250 g haricots verts or small string (French green) beans, cooked crisp-tender
1 medium red bell pepper (capsicum), roasted (see page 140) and cut into thin strips
½ lb/250 g cherry tomatoes, halved
½ cup/45 g/1½ oz Niçoise olives, halved and pitted
1 can (2 oz/60 g) anchovy fillets
2 tablespoons capers

Toss spaghettini with olive oil and salt and chill slightly.

Whisk all ingredients for dressing together and adjust seasonings.

Toss spaghettini again with about three-quarters of the dressing and arrange on serving platter or individual plates. Arrange tuna, eggs, beans, bell pepper, tomatoes and olives on pasta and top with anchovies, capers and remaining dressing. Serve at cool room temperature.

To Drink: This dish works best with a dry white wine such as a Sauvignon Blanc, a dry sparkler or a very light red.

**Available in Italian groceries or some supermarkets

Mostaccioli Salad with Swordfish

This is a wonderful buffet dish for a summer barbecue party, when the newly harvested garlic is at its freshest. Don't be put off by the large quantity of garlic: when baked, the "stinking rose" loses its pungency and takes on a sweet, nutty flavor.

½ lb/250 g mostaccioli, cooked (see page 10)
2 tablespoons olive oil
Salt to taste

Baked Garlic
2 to 4 medium bulbs garlic
¼ cup/60 mL/2 fl oz olive oil
Salt to taste

•

1 lb/500 g swordfish steak, 1 in/2.5 cm thick
1 tablespoon olive oil
½ tablespoon lemon juice

Mustard-Caper Dressing
4 to 6 cloves garlic, finely minced
½ cup/120 mL/4 fl oz olive oil
½ cup/120 mL/4 fl oz lemon juice
1 tablespoon finely minced or grated lemon zest
¼ cup/30 g/1 oz capers, drained
1 tablespoon Dijon-style mustard
¼ cup/45 g/1½ oz finely chopped red (Spanish) onion
½ cup/60 g/2 oz fresh parsley leaves, coarsely chopped
Salt and freshly ground pepper to taste

•

2 heads red leaf or other mild lettuce
Lemon wedges
Parsley sprigs

Toss mostaccioli with olive oil and salt and chill to desired temperature.

For Baked Garlic: Trim roots and loose papery membranes from garlic bulb. Place garlic on a large square of foil, drizzle with olive oil and sprinkle with salt. Wrap tightly, set in a baking dish and bake in a preheated oven (350°F/180°C/gas mark 4) until very soft, 1 to 1½ hours. Unwrap foil, allow garlic to cool slightly, peel individual cloves and refrigerate.

Dip swordfish in olive oil and lemon juice, coating fish evenly. Grill or broil until charred outside and rare at the center, about 2 to 3 minutes per side. Cool slightly, slice thinly and refrigerate.

For dressing: Whisk all ingredients together and adjust seasonings. Toss pasta with about three-quarters of the dressing and arrange on lettuce leaves on a serving platter. Arrange swordfish slices and baked garlic cloves on top; spoon remaining dressing over all and garnish with lemon and parsley. Serve slightly chilled.

To Drink: Serve a medium-weight white — a slightly herbal Sauvignon Blanc or citrusy Chardonnay — or a very light red, preferably chilled, such as a Beaujolais.

Crab Apple Salad

Here is a substantial luncheon dish or light summer supper, brimming with interesting contrasts of flavor and texture. In it, the natural sweetness of apple and orange balances the heat of the chile; the parsley complements the garlic and the smooth, thick aioli offsets the crisp crunch of peas, apple and onion. For an elegant presentation, serve the salad in individual crab shells.

½ lb/250 g maruzzine, cooked (see page 10)
2 tablespoons olive oil
Salt to taste

Crab Apple Mixture
¾ lb/375 g crabmeat (or "imitation" crabmeat)
1 medium green apple, skin on, finely chopped
¼ lb/120 g snow peas (mange tout), thinly sliced on the diagonal
½ cup/90 g/3 oz finely minced red (Spanish) onion
2 tablespoons lemon juice
1 small fresh hot red chile, finely minced (optional)
Salt and freshly ground white or black pepper to taste

Orange-Parsley Aioli
2 cups/500 mL/16 fl oz mayonnaise, preferably homemade (see page 139)
4 to 6 cloves garlic, finely minced
2 tablespoons orange juice concentrate
1 teaspoon finely minced or grated orange zest
¾ cup/90 g/3 oz fresh parsley leaves, plus extra for garnish

▪

2 heads lettuce, preferably red leaf or butter
Parsley sprigs

Toss cooked maruzzine with olive oil and salt and chill thoroughly.

Reserving about ¼ cup/45 g/1½ oz each of crab and snow peas for garnish, combine all ingredients for Crab Apple Mixture and chill.

For Orange-Parsley Aioli: Blend mayonnaise with garlic, orange juice concentrate, orange zest and parsley. (If using homemade mayonnaise, add these ingredients *before* blending in the olive oil.)

Combine pasta, Crab Apple Mixture and 1 cup/250 mL/8 fl oz of Orange-Parsley Aioli (or more to taste) and chill thoroughly. Adjust seasonings.

To serve, arrange lettuce on a serving platter, on individual salad plates or in well-washed individual crab shells. Spoon Crab Apple Salad on top. Garnish with reserved crab, snow peas and parsley sprigs. Serve well chilled.

To Drink: The spice and the sweetness of orange and apple would play off a fruity, slightly sweet Riesling, Gewürztraminer, Chenin Blanc or sparkling wine.

Pesce Tonnato on Pappardelle

This is an all-seafood twist on the classic Northern Italian vitello tonnato, or veal in tuna sauce. Serve it chilled, on a rustic-looking bed of wide pappardelle noodles, as an unusual – and unusually delicious – centerpiece for a summer buffet.

½ lb/250 g fresh pappardelle, (see page 137)
2 tablespoons extra-virgin olive oil
Salt to taste

Court Bouillon
1 cup/250 mL/8 fl oz dry white wine
1 cup water
¼ cup/60 mL/2 fl oz lemon juice
¼ cup/60 mL/2 fl oz olive oil
1 medium onion, coarsely chopped
2 medium carrots, coarsely chopped
1 medium stalk celery, coarsely chopped
4 sprigs fresh parsley
1 tablespoon coarsely chopped lemon zest
2 cloves

▪

1½ lb/750 g boneless shark, halibut or swordfish steak, 1 in/2.5 cm thick

Tuna Sauce
1 can (6 oz/185 g) oil-packed tuna, preferably Italian**
½ can (2 oz/60 g) anchovy fillets, drained
2 tablespoons capers
¼ cup/60 mL/2 fl oz extra-virgin olive oil
¼ cup/60 mL/2 fl oz lemon juice
¼ cup/30 g/1 oz fresh parsley leaves
1 to 2 cloves garlic, finely minced
½ cup/120 mL/4 fl oz mayonnaise, preferably homemade (see page 139)
Salt and freshly ground white or black pepper to taste

▪

Lemon slices, halved
Parsley sprigs

Combine all ingredients for Court Bouillon in a pan; cover and simmer 1 hour. Add fish and poach over low heat until barely cooked through, about 20 minutes. Chill fish in broth for several hours or overnight. Slice fish diagonally, across the grain, in very thin slices, and keep chilled. Reserve broth.

In a blender (liquidizer) or food processor, puree all ingredients for tuna sauce except mayonnaise until smooth. Blend in mayonnaise plus ½ cup/120 mL/4 fl oz broth (reserve remaining broth for another use); adjust seasonings and chill sauce.

Cook pappardelle (see page 10) about 2 minutes. Toss with olive oil and salt; chill. Toss again with about three-quarters of the tuna sauce and transfer to a serving platter. Arrange fish slices on pappardelle and spoon remaining sauce over fish. Garnish with lemon and parsley and serve chilled.

To Drink: Try a chilled white or sparkling wine with medium body for a refreshing counterpoint. Something from Northern Italy or a citrusy, slightly herbal Sauvignon Blanc would be ideal.

**Available in Italian groceries and some supermarkets

Pasta Salad from the Grill

This is definitely no ordinary pasta salad! You'll never go back to plain old noodles, mayonnaise and celery again. For an extra-quick dinner, you can make this dish any time you have leftover grilled or broiled salmon on hand, and feel free to vary the aioli with fresh herbs of your choice, such as basil, tarragon or parsley.

½ lb/250 g fusilli, cooked (see page 10)
2 tablespoons extra-virgin olive oil
Salt to taste
▪
1 lb/500 g salmon fillet or steak, grilled and cut into chunks (1 in/2.5 cm)
1 large red bell pepper (capsicum), grilled or roasted (see page 140)
1 large yellow bell pepper (capsicum), grilled or roasted (see page 140)
6 green (spring) onions, thinly sliced (white plus 2 in/5 cm green)
2 tablespoons extra-virgin olive oil
1 tablespoon lemon juice
Salt and freshly ground pepper to taste

Rosemary Aioli
1 cup/250 mL/8 fl oz mayonnaise, preferably homemade (see page 139)
2 to 4 cloves garlic, finely chopped
1 to 2 teaspoons finely minced fresh rosemary
6 cups/750 g/24 oz mixed young greens, well washed and dried

Toss cooked fusilli with olive oil and salt; chill well.

Combine salmon, grilled peppers, green onions, olive oil and lemon juice in a medium bowl. Adjust seasonings and refrigerate.

For Rosemary Aioli: Blend mayonnaise with garlic and rosemary.

Toss fusilli with Rosemary Aioli, then with salmon mixture. Chill well and serve cold on a bed of mixed greens.

To Drink: A light-bodied red, slightly chilled, a full-flavored Italian white such as a Verdicchio, or even a crisp, inexpensive sparkling wine, such as a Spanish cava, plays off the richness of the salmon and the garlicky mayonnaise.

Caribbean Conch Salad

*The calypso of colors, flavors and even the shapes of this summertime salad reflect
the spirit of the Caribbean. Complement the morsels of conch (say "conk") with conchiglie,
"conch shell" pasta, to complete this festive dish.*

¼ lb/120 g conchiglie

Pineapple-Lime Dressing
½ cup/120 mL/4 fl oz fresh, frozen or canned pineapple juice
½ cup/120 mL/4 fl oz lime juice (preferably Key limes)
½ cup/120 mL/4 fl oz olive oil
4 green (spring) onions, thinly sliced (white plus 2 in/5 cm green)
1 clove garlic, finely minced
1 to 2 small fresh hot red chiles, finely minced
¼ cup/20 g/¾ oz grated carrot
½ cup/60 g/2 oz cilantro (coriander) leaves, coarsely chopped
Salt and freshly ground pepper to taste

·

1 can (15 oz/450 g) conch (or "abalone-type shellfish"),
drained and coarsely chopped
1 small head dark green lettuce or 1 bunch spinach (English spinach),
washed and trimmed
1 avocado, thinly sliced lengthwise
1 medium grapefruit, preferably pink, halved and segmented
1 cup/120 g/4 oz fresh, frozen or canned pineapple,
drained and cut into small chunks
¼ medium cucumber, cut into thin sticks
½ medium red bell pepper (capsicum), sliced into thin rings
Cilantro (coriander) sprigs

Combine all ingredients for dressing and marinate conch at least ½ hour in the
refrigerator.

Cook conchiglie (see page 10) about 12 minutes. Toss pasta with about three-
quarters of the conch mixture and chill.

Arrange greens on a large serving platter and mound pasta mixture in the
center. Surround with avocado, grapefruit, pineapple, cucumber and bell pepper. Top with remaining conch mixture and cilantro sprigs. Serve chilled.

To Drink: Sweetness and spice — that calls for beer or a slightly sweet white wine
such as a Riesling, Gewürztraminer, Chenin Blanc, or even a good jug wine. An
off-dry bubbly would enhance the party mood.

New Zealand Mussel Salad

Say "kiwi" in New Zealand and you mean either a native, the national bird, or a green-fleshed fruit with fuzzy brown skin. This showstopping green-and-orange salad highlights the kiwifruit along with another highly prized New Zealand product, the greenlip mussel.

½ lb/250 g fresh spinach tagliarine, linguine or spaghetti, cooked (see page 137)

2 tablespoons olive oil

Salt to taste

•

3 dozen medium New Zealand greenlip mussels (about 2 lbs/1 kg)

½ cup/120 mL/4 fl oz water

Spicy Orange Dressing

½ cup/120 mL/4 fl oz olive oil

¼ cup/60 mL/2 fl oz lemon juice

1 tablespoon rice vinegar**

2 tablespoons orange juice concentrate

2 green (spring) onions, thinly sliced (white plus 2 in/5 cm green)

1 tablespoon finely minced Japanese-style pickled ginger** or fresh ginger juice, (see page 140), optional

1 teaspoon ground cumin

1 teaspoon dry mustard

1 teaspoon freshly ground black pepper

Salt to taste

•

2 medium oranges, peeled and thinly sliced

2 medium kiwifruit, peeled and thinly sliced

2 medium heads butter lettuce or other mild variety

Toss cooked pasta with olive oil and salt and refrigerate.

Steam mussels with water until they open, about 5 minutes. Strain and reserve liquid for another use. Chill mussels in refrigerator.

Whisk all ingredients for dressing together. Fold in mussels, oranges and kiwifruit and marinate in refrigerator 1 hour.

Just before serving, toss pasta with about three-quarters of the dressing and arrange on lettuce leaves. Arrange remaining oranges, kiwifruit and mussels over pasta and top with remaining dressing. Serve chilled.

To Drink: The intriguing contrasts of this dish work best with a slightly sweet white or sparkling wine. For a party, mix a mimosa punch with orange juice, sparkling wine and sliced kiwifruit garnish.

**Available in Asian groceries or some supermarkets

Rice Sticks with Butterfish and Tropical Fruit Relish

Both sweet and slightly oily, Pacific butterfish takes extremely well to this cool but spicy relish of tropical fruit and chiles. Chilled rice stick noodles absorb the flavors of both.

½ lb/250 g rice sticks,** soaked (see page 10)

■

1 lb/500 g butterfish or cod
½ tablespoon sesame oil**

Tropical Fruit Relish
½ medium papaya (pawpaw), peeled, seeded and cut into cubes (½ in/1 cm)
½ small honeydew or cantaloupe, cut into cubes (½ in/1 cm)
1 medium avocado, cut into cubes (½ in/1 cm)
½ cup/90 g/3 oz finely chopped red (Spanish) onion
½ cup/120 mL/4 fl oz lime juice
1 to 2 small fresh hot red chiles, finely minced
¼ cup/30 g/1 oz fresh cilantro (coriander) leaves, coarsely chopped
½ tablespoon sesame oil**
Salt to taste

Drain the rice sticks; rinse in cold water and chill.

Coat butterfish with sesame oil and steam over boiling water until just cooked through, about 8 to 10 minutes. Chill butterfish.

Combine all ingredients for Tropical Fruit Relish and chill. Toss rice sticks with about half the liquid from the relish. Top noodles with relish, butterfish and remaining liquid. Serve chilled.

To Drink: A sweet, fruity white or sparkling wine or a cold, refreshing beer is called for here.

**Available in Asian groceries or some supermarkets

Thai Noodle Salad

*This sweet-spicy melange gets a fresh-tasting lift from lime juice and cooling mint leaves.
You can make the dressing several hours ahead to blend flavors and save some time. If you
can find it, use the more pungent, licoricey Thai basil; if not, regular basil will do.*

³⁄₄ lb/375 g fresh Chinese-style noodles,** cooked (see page 10) and chilled
Thai Peanut Dressing
¼ cup/60 g/2 oz crunchy peanut butter
¼ cup/60 mL/2 fl oz lime juice
6 green (spring) onions, thinly sliced (white plus 2 in/5 cm green)
1 tablespoon peanut oil
1 tablespoon fish sauce** (nuoc mam or nam pla)
1 tablespoon soy sauce
2 to 4 cloves garlic, squeezed through a garlic press or very finely minced
1 tablespoon fresh ginger juice (see page 000)
½ to 1 teaspoon chili oil**
¼ cup/30 g/1 oz fresh cilantro (coriander) leaves, coarsely chopped
¼ cup/30 g/1 oz fresh Thai basil** or regular basil leaves, coarsely chopped
2 tablespoons fresh mint leaves, coarsely chopped
½ tablespoon light brown sugar
•
1 lb/500 g squid (calamari), cleaned and cut into rings (½ in/1 cm)
1 lb/500 g medium prawns, peeled and deveined
2 tablespoons lime juice
¼ teaspoon chili oil**
1 small head iceberg or romaine (Cos) lettuce, thinly sliced
1 medium cucumber, thinly sliced
1 medium carrot, grated
¼ cup/30 g/1 oz salted dry-roasted peanuts, chopped
Lime wedges
Cilantro (coriander), basil and mint sprigs

Combine all ingredients for dressing; let stand at least 1 hour to blend flavors.
Toss noodles with dressing and refrigerate.

Poach calamari and prawns in boiling water until they just start to change
color, about 20 seconds. Drain and rinse immediately in cold water; dry on
paper towels and toss with lime juice and chili oil. Chill well.

Just before serving, place lettuce on a serving platter and arrange cucumber
slices around the rim. Arrange noodles on greens. Arrange carrots, squid and
prawns on top. Sprinkle peanuts over all and garnish with lime wedges and
sprigs of cilantro, basil and mint. Serve chilled.

To Drink: A fairly light, fruity or slightly sweet white or sparkling wine or a
good cold beer would help temper the chili spice.

**Available in Asian groceries or some supermarkets

Warm Grilled Mackerel Salad

Mackerel, typically a rather oily or "fishy" fish, takes well to the mellow, deep flavors of sherry vinegar, soy sauce and nuts. Serve this warm salad as a buffet dish, a light luncheon entree or a prelude to a summer barbecue.

½ lb/250 g riso or orzo, cooked (see page 10)

∙

1 lb/500 g mackerel fillets, in 4 or 6 pieces
½ tablespoon almond, walnut or olive oil
½ tablespoon soy sauce

Sherry-Almond Vinaigrette
½ cup/120 mL/4 fl oz almond, walnut or olive oil
¼ cup/60 mL/2 fl oz sherry vinegar
1 tablespoon soy sauce
4 green (spring) onions, thinly sliced (white plus 2 in/5cm green)
1 clove garlic, finely minced
Salt and freshly ground white or black pepper to taste

∙

½ medium head iceberg lettuce, thinly sliced
1 medium carrot, grated
¼ cup/30 g/1 oz toasted almonds (see page 141), halved, slivered or chopped

Dip mackerel in almond oil and soy sauce and grill, barbecue or broil until just cooked through, about 3 to 4 minutes per side.

Whisk together all ingredients for Sherry-Almond Vinaigrette. Arrange lettuce on a large serving platter or individual salad plates and sprinkle carrot around the edges. Toss riso or orzo with about three-quarters of the dressing and arrange on lettuce. Arrange grilled mackerel on pasta; top with remaining dressing and sprinkle with almonds. Serve warm.

To Drink: A full-bodied white, such as a barrel-aged Sauvignon Blanc or Chardonnay; a chilled fino or manzanilla sherry; or a robust ale would bring out the rich, caramelized flavors of this dish. Or try a light red such as a Pinot Noir.

Tuscan White Bean Salad

Compare this dish with the Pasta Fazool' on page 64. Although both recipes use similar ingredients, they serve quite different purposes. Try this one on a hot summer's day as a stand-alone salad or, without the tuna, as a side dish for grilled fish. When the weather turns cold and blustery, serve the hearty, spicy Pasta Fazool' instead. In either case, if you're starting from scratch with dried rather than canned beans, be sure to plan on soaking them overnight. Use canned, and this salad qualifies as "extra quick."

¼ lb/120 g ditalini, cooked (see page 10)

∎

1 can (15 oz/450 g) cannellini beans** (white kidney beans)
4 anchovy fillets, drained and finely chopped or mashed
½ cup/90 g/3 oz finely chopped red (Spanish) onion
2 cloves garlic, finely minced
½ tablespoon fresh rosemary, finely minced
½ cup/60 g/2 oz fresh parsley leaves, coarsely chopped
¼ cup/60 mL/2 fl oz extra-virgin olive oil
1 tablespoon lemon juice
Salt and freshly ground pepper to taste
1 can (7 oz/210 g) oil-packed tuna, preferably Italian,** flaked (optional)

Fold beans together with ditalini in a large serving bowl.

Combine remaining ingredients except for tuna; stir into beans and pasta; adjust seasonings and chill slightly. Top with tuna if desired and serve at cool room temperature.

To Drink: Any pleasantly tart, medium-to-full-bodied white or sparkling wine or light-bodied red will fill the bill with this very versatile salad.

**Available in Italian groceries and some supermarkets

Skate Salad

Divers and snorkelers will recognize the graceful skate, or ray, its rippling, fan-shaped wings gliding along the ocean floor. These wings are not only edible but quite delicious. Nibble on the bite-sized segments, and their sweet, mild flesh flakes easily off the thin cartilage.

½ lb/250 g acini di pepe or other tiny pasta

•

½ cup/120 g/4 oz lentils
2 tablespoons balsamic vinegar
¼ cup/60 mL/2 fl oz olive oil
Salt to taste
1 lb/500 g eggplant (aubergine), preferably the Asian variety, halved or quartered

•

½ lb/250 g skate wings, cut between cartilaginous "bones" into "fingers" 1 in/2.5 cm wide
2 tablespoons olive oil
½ cup/120 mL/4 fl oz white wine
Salt to taste

Rosemary-Balsamic Vinaigrette
¼ cup/60 mL/2 fl oz balsamic vinegar
½ cup/120 mL/4 fl oz extra-virgin olive oil
4 green (spring) onions, thinly sliced (white plus 2 in/5 cm green)
¼ cup/30 g/1 oz fresh parsley leaves, coarsely chopped
½ tablespoon finely minced fresh rosemary
Salt and freshly ground pepper to taste

Wash lentils and simmer in 1½ cups/375 mL/12 fl oz water until tender, about 1 to 1¼ hours. Drain if necessary and chill slightly.

Whisk together balsamic vinegar, olive oil and salt and pour some on a plate. Dip cut surfaces of eggplant in this mixture and place in a roasting pan. Roast eggplant in a preheated oven (375°F/190°C/gas mark 5) until tender and slightly browned, about 1 hour. Chill slightly.

Sauté skate wings in olive oil over low-medium heat, turning frequently, until just cooked through, about 2 to 3 minutes. Add wine, raise heat to high and cook until liquid reduces by about half. Drain and reserve liquid. Adjust seasonings and chill skate slightly.

Cook pasta (see page 10) about 5 minutes.

Whisk together all ingredients for vinaigrette. Add reserved skate liquid and adjust seasonings.

Arrange eggplant on a large platter. Top with pasta and spoon about one-third dressing evenly on top. Top with lentils and spoon on another one-third dressing. Top with skate and remaining dressing. Serve slightly chilled.

To Drink: This dish, with its robust flavors, can handle a full-flavored white or a light red such as a Beaujolais or Pinot Noir.

*Shrimp and Artichoke Farfalle Salad

Here's an incredibly fast way to make a meal just by digging around in the pantry. A few jars, a few cans, some onions, garlic and seasonings — and dinner is served!

½ lb/250 g farfalle, cooked (see page 10)

∙

2 jars (6 oz/185 g) marinated artichoke hearts
½ lb/250 g cooked fresh or canned tiny shrimp
1 cup/90 g/3 oz halved pitted canned ripe olives
½ cup/45 g/1½ oz roasted red bell pepper (capsicum), see page 140,
coarsely chopped
¼ cup/30 g/1 oz fresh parsley leaves, coarsely chopped
¼ cup/60 mL/2 fl oz lemon juice
2 tablespoons balsamic or other flavorful vinegar
½ medium red (Spanish) onion, finely minced
2 cloves garlic, finely minced
2 tablespoons Dijon-style mustard
1 teaspoon dried oregano
Salt and freshly ground pepper to taste

Drain artichoke hearts, reserving marinade, and chop coarsely. Toss farfalle with marinade.

In a separate bowl, combine shrimp with remaining ingredients, including artichokes. Toss pasta with shrimp mixture and adjust seasonings. Chill slightly before serving.

To Drink: Any simple light- to medium-bodied white will taste just fine with this easygoing summer fare.

ENTREES

Y ou've welcomed your guests into your home with a glass of wine and a savory appetizer or two. Or you've brought your family to the table with a tempting bowl of soup or refreshing salad. The conversation livens. Anticipation mounts. Everyone is waiting eagerly — for the main course. The *pièce de résistance:* the focus of your culinary creativity and, most likely, the dish that will make this meal memorable.

Your entree can be as simple or as sophisticated as your time, energy and budget permit. It can stand alone, or it can be the high point of an elaborate, multi-course feast.

Given the universal appeal of pasta, noodles, fish and shellfish of every description, you're bound to please with the main dish recipes that follow. There is literally a world of choices offered here, from a spicy Italian Penne Arrabbiata con Cozze to a rich, Hungarian Perch Paprikash; from a buttery Vietnamese Garlic-Pepper Prawns to a pecan-crunchy Cajun Catfish that echoes the Louisiana bayous.

Some of the dishes are classics of yesteryear — like Aunt Anna's Baked Ziti alle Sarde — others, such as Szechuan Noodles with Opakapaka, add novel ingredients to traditional combinations to create new classics in your kitchen. Still others pair seafood and pasta in totally original and exciting ways — Fettuccine with Scallops and Pears in Garlic-Ginger Cream Sauce, for example. The flavors can be subtle as a whisper, as in the delicate Linguine with Clam Sauce, or bold and assertive, as in the East-West-spiced Seared Ahi with Wasabi-Ginger Beurre Rouge. What's more, many of these recipes, such as Greek Baked Prawns and Crab-Spinach Cannelloni, make great fix-ahead party dishes you can pack to a potluck or pop in the oven when you're expecting a crowd. Several, like the Halibut with Ziti and Olive-Rosemary Tapenade, and Pappardelle with Swordfish, Tomatoes and Onions, make great use of your barbecue for relaxed outdoor entertaining.

Whichever you choose, just be sure to make enough for second helpings!

Shells with Asparagus, Crab and Cheese Fondue

Cheese fondue — creamy, rich and delicious with nothing more than cubes of crusty bread — reaches new heights when teamed with crab, asparagus and pasta. Bring this dish to a potluck (you can reheat it when you arrive), and it will be one of the first to disappear!

½ lb/250 g maruzzine, cooked (see page 10)

•

1 cup/250 mL/8 fl oz Fish Stock (see page 139)
1 cup/250 mL/8 fl oz dry white wine
1 clove garlic, finely minced
2 tablespoons lemon juice
1 tablespoon finely minced or grated lemon zest
1 lb/500 g Swiss (Gruyère) cheese, grated
1 tablespoon all-purpose (plain) flour
2 tablespoons kirsch or brandy (optional)
½ teaspoon ground nutmeg, plus extra for garnish
½ teaspoon freshly ground white or black pepper, or to taste
Salt to taste

•

½ lb/250 g asparagus tips, cooked crisp-tender and halved lengthwise
¾ lb/375 g crabmeat (or "imitation" crab)

Simmer stock, wine, garlic, lemon juice and zest for 10 minutes to blend flavors and evaporate alcohol. Toss cheese with flour and stir it gradually into the sauce. Add kirsch, if used, nutmeg, pepper and salt and simmer, stirring, 2 to 3 minutes. Adjust seasonings.

Toss maruzzine with about half the fondue sauce and arrange half the pasta in a baking dish. Top with half the asparagus and half the crab, then add the remaining pasta, asparagus and crab. Pour remaining fondue sauce over all and dust with additional nutmeg.

Bake, uncovered, in a preheated oven (400°F/200°C/gas mark 6) until golden and bubbly, about 10 to 15 minutes. Serve hot.

To Drink: A big, buttery Chardonnay or full-flavored sparkling wine will bring out the richness here; or follow tradition and serve a slightly sweet Riesling.

Pecan-Chili-Crusted Flounder

Although the inspiration for this dish is Southwest USA, the pecans bring a touch of the Deep South. Regardless, it's a lively, spicy melange guaranteed to bring sweat to your brow.

¾ lb/375 g stelle or other small pasta

•

½ cup/30 g/1 oz bread crumbs (preferably from corn bread)
2 to 3 tablespoons ground dried New Mexico chiles or other medium-hot ground chile pepper, or to taste
½ cup/60 g/2 oz finely minced pecans
Salt and freshly ground white or black pepper to taste
1 lb/500 g flounder (flat white fish), in 4 to 6 fillets
1 to 2 egg whites, beaten
½ cup/120 mL/4 fl oz olive oil, divided
6 tablespoons/90 g/3 oz butter, divided

•

6 green (spring) onions, thinly sliced (white plus 2 in/5 cm green)
6 to 8 cloves garlic, finely minced
1 to 2 small fresh hot red chiles, finely minced
1½ cups/375 mL/12 fl oz good-quality beer
¼ cup/60 mL/2 fl oz lemon juice
1½ cups/250 g/8 oz fresh or frozen corn
1 cup/120 g/4 oz fresh cilantro (coriander) leaves, coarsely chopped
Salt and freshly ground white or black pepper to taste

•

Cilantro (coriander) sprigs
Lemon wedges

Combine bread crumbs, ground chile pepper, pecans, salt and pepper. Dip flounder in egg white, then in seasoned bread crumbs, coating flounder on both sides and patting coating on well. Sauté flounder in half the olive oil and one-half the butter over medium heat, until coating turns golden and fish cooks through, about 1 to 2 minutes per side. Add any remaining bread crumb mixture and sauté along with fish. Remove flounder and keep warm.

Cook stelle (see page 10) about 5 minutes.

Meanwhile, sauté green onions, garlic and fresh chiles in remaining olive oil and butter over low-medium heat until soft and fragrant, about 3 to 5 minutes. Raise heat to medium-high; add beer, lemon juice and corn and cook until corn is tender and liquid reduces by about half, about 3 to 5 minutes. Stir in cilantro and adjust seasonings.

Toss stelle with about three-quarters of the sauce; top with flounder, remaining sauce and any remaining bread crumb mixture. Garnish with cilantro and lemon and serve hot.

To Drink: This dish is so spicy that you'll probably want to wash it down with beer. Diehard wine lovers should choose a rather sweet, fruity white.

Tagliarine con Polpette di Pesce

*With a delicate white sauce, these light seafood polpette (meatballs) and citrus-zesty pasta
are a far cry – and a welcome change – from garden-variety spaghetti and meatballs.*

**1 lb/500 g fresh lemon or plain tagliarine, preferably homemade
(see page 137)**

Seafood Polpette
½ lb/250 g cod or other firm-fleshed white fish, coarsely chopped
½ lb/250 g raw prawns, peeled, deveined and coarsely chopped
½ cup/30 g/1 oz unseasoned bread crumbs
2 egg whites
2 green (spring) onions, finely chopped (white plus 2 in/5 cm green)
Salt and freshly ground white or black pepper to taste
■
2 tablespoons olive oil
2 tablespoons/30 g/1 oz butter
1 cup/250 mL/8 fl oz dry white wine
1 cup/250 mL/8 fl oz Fish Stock (see page 139)
2 tablespoons lemon juice
1 tablespoon finely minced lemon zest
¼ cup/30 g/1oz fresh tarragon leaves, coarsely chopped
Salt and freshly ground white or black pepper to taste

Combine all ingredients for Seafood Polpette in a food processor or blender
(liquidizer) and process, using rapid pulses, until mixture is well blended but still
slightly chunky. Chill mixture thoroughly. Form mixture into balls (1 in/2.5 cm)
and sauté in olive oil and butter over medium heat. Shake pan frequently to cook
all sides evenly, until polpette are slightly golden outside and just cooked through,
about 3 to 5 minutes. Remove polpette with a slotted spoon and keep warm.

Cook tagliarine (see page 10) about 2 minutes.

Meanwhile, add wine to pan; raise heat to high and cook until liquid reduces
by about half. Stir in remaining ingredients and simmer 2 to 3 minutes to blend
flavors. Adjust seasonings.

Toss pasta with sauce; top with polpette and serve hot.

To Drink: A medium- to full-bodied white wine with either buttery flavors, such
as a Chardonnay, or crisp acidity and herbal flavors, such as a Sauvignon Blanc,
could have different, but equally interesting effects here.

*Lemon-Pepper Fettuccine with Scallops and Sun-Dried Tomatoes

This quick-cooking showstopper never fails to draw raves with its vibrant, sophisticated colors and flavors. Serve it when time is at a premium — you'll not only impress your guests, but you'll have lots more time to enjoy their company!

**1 lb/500 g fresh lemon-pepper or plain fettuccine,
preferably homemade (see page 137)**

·

1 lb/500 g large sea scallops, sliced horizontally ½ in/1 cm thick
½ cup/120 mL/4 fl oz olive oil, divided
2 to 4 cloves garlic, finely minced
½ cup/120 mL/4 fl oz dry white wine
½ cup/90 g/3 oz oil-packed sun-dried tomatoes, drained and coarsely chopped
¼ cup/30 g/1 oz fresh parsley leaves, coarsely chopped
2 tablespoons capers
2 tablespoons lemon juice
½ tablespoon finely minced or grated lemon zest
Salt and freshly ground white or black pepper to taste

Sauté scallop slices in half the olive oil over medium heat, stirring constantly, until just cooked through, about 1 to 2 minutes. Remove and reserve scallops and their cooking liquid.

Add remaining olive oil to pan and sauté garlic over low-medium heat, stirring often, until soft and fragrant, about 3 to 5 minutes.

Cook fettuccine (see page 10) about 2 minutes.

Meanwhile, add wine to sautéed garlic, raise heat to high and cook until liquid reduces by about half. Stir in remaining ingredients; return scallops and their liquid to pan and heat through. Adjust seasonings.

Toss pasta with about three-quarters of the sauce; top with scallops and remaining sauce and serve hot.

To Drink: A crisp, slightly herbal Sauvignon Blanc picks up nicely on all the tangy flavors in this dish, but any dry white wine with medium body and good acidity will also do it justice.

Cajun Catfish

The curly noodles used in this dish, sometimes called mafalde, look like long, thin slices trimmed from ruffle-edged lasagne. In this Louisiana-style recipe, the ruffles hold the spicy sauce and pecan nuggets while adding a texture all their own.

½ lb/250 g mafalde

•

¼ cup/45 g/1½ oz cornmeal (fine polenta/maize)
½ teaspoon cayenne
¼ teaspoon salt, or to taste
Freshly ground white or black pepper to taste
1 lb/500 g catfish fillets
2 egg whites, beaten
4 tablespoons/60 g/2 oz butter
2 tablespoons olive oil
1 medium onion, finely chopped
2 cloves garlic, finely minced
¼ cup/30 g/1 oz coarsely chopped pecans
½ cup/120 mL/4 fl oz beer
1 cup/250 mL/8 fl oz Fish Stock (see page 139)
¼ cup/60 mL/2 fl oz lemon juice
1 tablespoon sweet ground paprika
1 teaspoon cayenne, or to taste
Salt and freshly ground white or black pepper to taste

•

Parsley sprigs
Lemon wedges

Combine cornmeal with cayenne, salt and pepper. Dip catfish in egg whites, then in seasoned cornmeal. Sauté in butter over medium heat until crust is golden and fish is just cooked through, about 3 to 4 minutes per side. Remove catfish and keep warm.

Add olive oil and onions to pan and sauté over medium heat, until onions are soft and translucent, about 5 to 7 minutes. Stir in garlic and pecans and sauté until garlic is soft and fragrant. Add beer, raise heat to high, and cook until liquid reduces by about half. Stir in remaining ingredients; lower heat and simmer 15 minutes, stirring occasionally. Adjust seasonings.

About 10 minutes before the sauce has finished simmering, cook the mafalde (see page 10) about 12 minutes.

Toss pasta with about three-quarters of the sauce in a serving bowl. Arrange catfish over pasta and top with remaining sauce. Garnish with parsley and lemon wedges and serve hot.

To Drink: In bayou country, a frosty beer would be the drink of choice — but don't let that stop you from trying a cool fruity white wine to tame the flames.

Aunt Anna's Baked Ziti alle Sarde

Zia Anna, one of my grandma Rose's many talented sisters, was an absolute master of the exotic, Arab-influenced cuisine of Sicily. This unusual holiday dish, re-created from my childhood memory, was a personal favorite. If you use fresh sardines, as she did, try to find tiny ones whose bones fall apart during cooking.

1 lb/500 g ziti
¼ cup/60 mL/2 fl oz olive oil
Salt to taste
▪
3 medium onions, thinly sliced
1 cup/250 mL/8 fl oz olive oil, divided
4 cloves garlic, finely minced
2 bulbs fresh fennel (anise), stalks removed, thinly sliced
1 cup/250 mL/8 fl oz dry white wine
1 can (2 oz/60 g) anchovy fillets, drained and finely chopped
¼ cup/45 g/1½ oz golden raisins (sultanas)
¼ cup/30 g/1 oz pine nuts (kernels)
½ cup/60 g/2 oz fresh parsley leaves, coarsely chopped
**1 lb/500 g very small fresh sardines, head and tail removed, cleaned or
2 cans (4 oz/125 g) oil-packed sardines, drained and mashed**
Salt and freshly ground pepper to taste

Sauté onions in half the olive oil over medium heat until soft and translucent, about 10 to 15 minutes. When onions are almost done, stir in garlic and sauté until soft and fragrant. Add fennel and white wine; cover and cook until fennel is crisp-tender, about 5 minutes. Stir in anchovies, raisins, pine nuts and parsley.

For fresh sardines: Sauté in remaining olive oil over medium heat until just cooked through, about 2 to 3 minutes per side. Separate meat carefully from backbone and mash with a fork, removing tiny bones. Stir into fennel mixture and adjust seasonings. If using canned sardines, simply mash them, bones and all. (You will not need the remaining olive oil.)

Meanwhile, cook the ziti (see page 10) about 12 minutes. Toss with olive oil and salt and layer about one-third of it into a baking dish. Top with about one-third of the sardine-fennel sauce. Continue layering remaining pasta and sauce. Cover tightly and bake in a preheated oven (375°F/190°C/gas mark 5) until heated through, about 20 minutes. Serve hot.

To Drink: Either a medium-to-full-bodied white or a fruity, light red can work here — but to enhance the holiday spirit, try a not-too-dry sparkling wine.

Penne with Lobster, Scallops and Asparagus

With such precious commodities as lobster, scallops and asparagus, and liberal lashings of butter, this recipe is one of the richest in this book. Life is short — indulge yourself!

1 lb/500 g penne rigate

▪

2 lobsters (1½ lb/750 g each)
1 lb/500 g medium scallops
¼ lb/120 g shallots, finely minced
4 tablespoons/60 g/2 oz butter
¾ cup/185 mL/6 fl oz dry white wine
½ cup/120 mL/4 fl oz heavy (double) cream
2 tablespoons fresh tarragon leaves
2 tablespoons lemon juice
½ tablespoon finely minced or grated lemon zest
¾ lb/375 g asparagus tips (2 in/5 cm)
Salt and freshly ground white or black pepper to taste

Steam or boil lobsters 10 to 12 minutes; cool slightly and break off tail and claws. Remove tail and claw meat from shells; slice tail meat thinly. Reserve liquid that drains from the lobsters as you break them apart.

Cook the penne rigate (see page 10) about 12 minutes.

Meanwhile, over medium heat, sauté scallops and shallots in butter until barely cooked, about 2 to 3 minutes. Remove and reserve scallops. Add wine and reduce by half. Add heavy cream, tarragon, lemon juice, lemon zest and enough reserved lobster liquid to make a creamy consistency, about ½ cup (120 mL/4 fl oz) or more. Reduce slightly and adjust seasonings.

Steam or boil asparagus until crisp-tender, about 5 minutes. Add lobster, scallops and asparagus to sauce and heat through. Toss with pasta and serve hot.

To Drink: To echo the full flavors and buttery opulence of this dish, serve your biggest and best Chardonnay or a rich, high-quality sparkling wine. Cheers!

L O B S T E R

Fettuccine Alfredo with Lobster

Sorry, dieters. Here's another rich, rich lobster dish. Enjoy it while you may,
for tomorrow is another day.

1 lb/500 g fresh fettuccine (see page 137)

▪

2 live lobsters (1½ lb/375 g each)
½ cup/120 g/4 oz butter, softened
1 cup/250 mL/8 fl oz heavy (double) cream, warmed
1 cup/185 g/6 oz freshly grated parmesan cheese
½ cup/60 g/2 oz fresh parsley leaves, coarsely chopped
¼ teaspoon freshly ground white or black pepper, or to taste
Salt to taste

Boil or steam lobsters 10 to 12 minutes; cool slightly, break apart, and carefully
remove and reserve meat from tail, body and claws. Also reserve coral (orange-
colored roe) if present, tomalley (green-colored liver), liquid and creamy white
material from body shell. Keep claw meat whole if possible; slice tail thinly and
finely chop remaining meat.

Cook fettuccine (see page 10) about 2 minutes.

Meanwhile, in a large skillet, over medium heat, toss pasta with butter,
cream, parmesan and enough of the lobster liquid to make a creamy sauce
(½ cup/120 mL/4 fl oz, or more); fold in parsley, chopped lobster meat, coral
and other extras. Adjust seasonings. Place pasta on a large serving platter and
arrange lobster claws and tail meat slices on top. Serve hot.

To Drink: Since you've splurged on the lobsters, why not splurge on a top-notch
Chardonnay, or a good sparkler — or a true Champagne. You deserve it!

QUADRILLE

Fettuccine with Scallops and Pears in Garlic-Ginger Cream Sauce

Strange as it may seem, the combination of scallops and pears works beautifully. Both have natural sweetness, which is enhanced by the sesame oil, ginger and cream — and their contrasting smooth and crunchy textures add great appeal. If you can't find lemon verbena, a perennial herb with an intense lemon flavor, substitute lemon thyme or use flat-leaf Italian parsley plus 1 teaspoon grated lemon zest.

½ lb/250 g fresh fettuccine (see page 137)

∎

6 cloves garlic, sliced
4 tablespoons butter
1 tablespoon sesame oil**
1 lb/500 g sea scallops, halved horizontally
½ cup/120 mL/4 fl oz dry white wine
1 tablespoon lemon juice
1 large ripe pear, cored and diced
¼ cup/60 mL/2 fl oz heavy (double) cream
4 large sprigs lemon verbena
2 tablespoons fresh ginger juice (see page 140)
Salt and freshly ground white or black pepper to taste

∎

Lemon wedges
Lemon verbena sprigs

Sauté garlic in butter and sesame oil over medium heat until it just starts to become translucent, about 2 minutes. Add scallop slices and sauté, stirring or shaking pan frequently, until scallops become white and opaque, about 2 to 3 minutes. Remove scallops and set aside.

Cook fettuccine (see page 10) about 2 minutes.

Meanwhile, using the same pan as for scallops, turn heat to high and add wine and lemon juice. Cook until liquid reduces by about half. Stir in pear, cream, lemon verbena and ginger; cook briefly to thicken sauce slightly and blend flavors. Stir in scallops and heat through. Remove lemon verbena and adjust seasonings.

Pour sauce over fettuccine and toss gently, coating pasta evenly and keeping scallops and pears on top. Serve hot, garnishing serving platter or individual portions with lemon wedges and herb sprigs.

To Drink: Fruity, off-dry white wines such as Rieslings, Gewürztraminers, Chenin Blancs or slightly sweet sparklers do extremely well with spicy-sweet East-West combos such as this.

**Available in Asian groceries or some supermarkets

*Vermicelli alla Puttanesca

There's a good reason why this sauce is so speedy to fix. Reputedly (or ill-reputedly, if you prefer), it was devised by Italian prostitutes (puttane), who could whip up a quick batch in between customers — and still have time to fluff up the pillows.

1 lb/500 g vermicelli

·

4 to 6 cloves garlic, finely minced
¼ cup/60 mL/2 fl oz olive oil
4 cups/1 kg/2 lb finely chopped fresh or canned tomatoes
¼ cup/20 g/¾ oz halved and pitted Niçoise, Kalamata or other flavorful olives
2 tablespoons capers
1 teaspoon dried oregano
1 teaspoon dried hot red pepper flakes, or to taste
½ teaspoon freshly ground black pepper, or to taste
1 can (2 oz/60 g) anchovy fillets, drained and finely chopped
¼ cup/30 g/1 oz fresh parsley leaves, coarsely chopped
Salt to taste

Cook vermicelli (see page 10) about 5 minutes.

Meanwhile, sauté garlic in olive oil over medium heat, stirring often, until fragrant and golden, about 3 to 5 minutes. Stir in tomatoes, olives, capers, oregano, and red and black pepper, and simmer until slightly thickened, about 10 to 15 minutes. Stir in anchovies and parsley and simmer 2 minutes. Adjust seasonings. Toss pasta with sauce and serve hot.

To Drink: In keeping with this dish's racy origins, pour tumblers of any red wine you consider — well — lusty!

Spaghetti con Calamari

Calamari, or squid, are as delicious, nutritious, versatile and inexpensive as they are, alas, unpopular. True, they turn to rubber if you overcook them, and they're a bit of a bother to clean, but their wonderful, sweet flavor is certainly worth the slight extra effort!

1 lb/500 g spaghetti

■

6 cloves garlic, finely minced
½ cup/120 mL/4 fl oz olive oil, divided
4 cups/1 kg/2 lb fresh or canned pureed tomatoes
½ cup/120 mL/4 fl oz dry red wine
¼ cup/30 g/1 oz fresh parsley leaves, coarsely chopped
¼ cup/30 g/1 oz fresh basil leaves, coarsely chopped
2 lb/1 kg squid (calamari), cleaned and cut into rings
Salt and freshly ground pepper to taste

Sauté garlic in half the olive oil over low-medium heat, stirring often, until soft and fragrant, about 5 to 7 minutes. Stir in tomatoes and wine and simmer, uncovered, until sauce thickens, about 30 minutes.

Halfway through, cook the spaghetti (see page 10) about 10 minutes.

Add parsley and basil to sauce and simmer 5 minutes longer.

In a separate pan, sauté squid in remaining olive oil until color just begins to change, about 1 to 2 minutes. Stir into tomato sauce and adjust seasonings.

Toss pasta with half the sauce; pour remaining sauce and squid on top and serve hot.

To Drink: With red wine built into the sauce, red wine in the glass is a natural. Choose something light and rustic — a Valpolicella, Beaujolais or Zinfandel.

Penne Arrabbiata con Cozze

Arrabbiata, meaning "angry," is an apt description of this fiery combination.
If this much ire isn't quite your style, just cut back on the hot pepper.

1 lb/500 g penne

·

3 dozen medium mussels (about 2 lbs/1 kg)
½ cup/120 mL/4 fl oz dry white wine or water
6 cloves garlic, finely minced
¼ cup/60 mL/2 fl oz olive oil
2 tablespoons/30 g/1 oz butter
4 cups/1 kg/2 lb fresh or canned pureed tomatoes
½ to 1 teaspoon dried hot red pepper flakes, or to taste
¼ cup/30 g/1 oz fresh basil leaves, coarsely chopped
¼ cup/30 g/1 oz fresh parsley leaves, coarsely chopped
Salt and freshly ground pepper to taste

Steam mussels with wine until open, about 5 minutes. Strain; reserve liquid.

Sauté garlic in olive oil and butter over medium heat, stirring often, until it turns fragrant and golden brown, about 3 to 5 minutes. Add tomatoes, reserved mussel liquid (about 1 cup/250 mL/8 fl oz) and hot pepper. Simmer, uncovered, until sauce thickens, about 30 minutes.

Halfway through, cook penne (see page 10) about 12 minutes.

Stir basil and parsley into sauce; simmer 5 minutes longer. Add mussels and heat through. Adjust seasonings.

Toss penne with half the sauce; top with remaining sauce and mussels and serve hot.

To Drink: A medium- to full-bodied white or sparkling wine will cool the flames of the hot pepper, or try a light, fruity red such as a Beaujolais, Valpolicella or light Zinfandel.

Bucatini all'Amatriciana

This classic dish from the town of Amatrice, in the Sabine hills outside Rome, is a must-try in trattorie throughout the region. The original, often made with long, tubular bucatini, contains pancetta (unsmoked bacon) but no seafood. I've added tender ocean perch — but feel free to substitute any freshly caught fish.

1 lb/500 g bucatini, cooked (see page 10)

∎

4 slices pancetta or lean bacon, cut into strips (¼ in/.5 cm)
¼ cup/60 mL/2 fl oz olive oil
1 medium onion, finely chopped
½ teaspoon dried hot red pepper flakes, or to taste
4 cups/1 kg/2 lb fresh or canned tomatoes, drained, seeded and chopped
1½ lb/750 g ocean perch or rockfish (red snapper) fillets, cut into strips (1 in/2.5 cm)
Salt and freshly ground pepper to taste
½ cup/90 g/3 oz grated pecorino (sheep's milk) or parmesan cheese

Sauté pancetta in olive oil over medium heat, stirring frequently, until softened and slightly translucent, about 3 minutes. Add onion and hot pepper and cook, stirring, until onion turns soft and translucent, about 5 to 7 minutes.

Meanwhile, cook the bucatini (see page 10) about 12 minutes.

Stir in tomatoes and cook, stirring, until sauce thickens slightly, about 10 minutes.

Stir the fish into the sauce and cook until just done, about 2 minutes. Adjust seasonings. Toss pasta with sauce and half the cheese. Serve hot, and pass the remaining cheese.

To Drink: With the meaty bacon and spicy red pepper, look for a light-to-medium-bodied red such as a Chianti, or even a Spanish Rioja. Just steer clear of a light-bodied white — the zesty flavors of this sauce will make it taste like water!

Mostaccioli con Gamberi e Broccoli al Pesto

This recipe teams a classic basil pesto with several not-so-classic partners: plump pink prawns, deep-green broccoli nuggets and bias-cut "mustache" macaroni.

½ lb/250 g mostaccioli

∎

½ lb/250 g broccoli florets
1 lb/500 g medium prawns, shelled and deveined
¼ cup/60 mL/2 fl oz olive oil
¼ cup/60 mL/2 fl oz dry white wine
½ cup/120 mL/4 fl oz Fish Stock (see page 139)
2 tablespoons lemon juice
Salt and freshly ground pepper to taste

Pesto
2 cups/250 g/8 oz fresh basil leaves
½ cup/60 mL/2 fl oz olive oil
¼ cup/30 g/1 oz pine nuts (kernels)
4 cloves garlic, chopped
1 cup/185 g/6 oz freshly grated parmesan cheese, divided
Salt and freshly ground pepper to taste

Cook mostaccioli (see page 10) about 12 minutes.

Meanwhile, steam broccoli crisp-tender and reserve.

Sauté prawns in olive oil over medium heat, stirring, until cooked through, about 3 minutes. Raise heat to high; add wine and cook, stirring, until alcohol evaporates and liquid reduces by about half, about 2 to 3 minutes longer. Lower heat to medium; add Fish Stock and lemon juice and heat through. Adjust seasonings, stir in broccoli and heat through. Spoon out liquid and reserve.

Combine first four pesto ingredients in a blender (liquidizer) or food processor and puree until smooth. Blend in half the parmesan cheese and the cooking liquid from prawns. If sauce is too thick, add some hot water, a tablespoon at a time, to thin it. Warm sauce if necessary and adjust seasonings.

Toss mostaccioli with about three-quarters of the pesto sauce and transfer to a serving platter. Arrange prawns and broccoli on top. Spoon remaining pesto over prawns and broccoli. Serve hot, and pass the remaining parmesan.

To Drink: A crisp medium-bodied dry white or sparkling wine cuts through the prawns, cheese and olive oil, setting up your taste buds for another bite.

Capellini con Cozze

When I make this dish, I always think back to a magical afternoon I spent with friends on the beach at Bodega Bay, north of San Francisco. As the bivalve brigade rushed to gather mussels in the incoming tide, the campfire crew heated a pot of freshly cooked tomato sauce I'd brought from home over a driftwood blaze. We washed our mussels – several gallons' worth – in the surf and steamed them open in a kettle of sea water. Every morsel was gone in five minutes!

1 lb/500 g capellini or capelli d'angelo

·

4 dozen medium mussels (about 3 lbs/1.5 kg)
½ cup/120 mL/4 fl oz dry white wine or water
4 sprigs fresh parsley
2 cloves garlic, crushed
½ medium onion, sliced

Tomato Sauce
½ medium onion, finely chopped
¼ cup/60 mL/2 fl oz olive oil
2 cloves garlic, finely minced
4 cups/1 kg/2 lb chopped or pureed fresh or canned tomatoes
2 to 3 roasted red bell peppers (capsicums), see page 140, coarsely chopped
½ cup/45 g/1½ oz, pitted Niçoise, Kalamata or other flavorful olives, coarsely chopped
½ cup/60 g/2 oz fresh parsley leaves, coarsely chopped
½ cup/60 g/2 oz fresh basil leaves, coarsely chopped
2 tablespoons fresh marjoram or oregano leaves, coarsely chopped
¼ to ½ teaspoon dried hot red pepper flakes (optional)
Salt and freshly ground pepper to taste

Steam mussels with wine, parsley, garlic and onion until they open, about 5 minutes. Strain and reserve liquid. (To serve this dish without shells, scoop out mussel meats into a small bowl, pinching off any remaining traces of beard.)

For Tomato Sauce: Sauté onions in olive oil over medium heat until soft and translucent, about 5 to 7 minutes. When onions are almost done, stir in garlic and sauté until soft and fragrant. Stir in tomatoes, roasted peppers and olives and simmer, stirring frequently, for about 30 minutes or until sauce thickens slightly.

About two-thirds through, cook capellini (see page 10) about 5 minutes.

Meanwhile, stir parsley, basil, about ¾ cup/180 mL/6 fl oz of the mussel liquid (reserve remainder for another use) and red pepper flakes, if used, into the sauce. Simmer 5 minutes longer and adjust seasonings. Stir in mussels and heat through.

Toss capellini with half the sauce and arrange mussels over pasta. Top with remaining sauce and serve hot.

To Drink: This hearty red tomato sauce can handle a light but rustic red wine — an inexpensive Chianti, a Beaujolais or a light-style Zinfandel. If you prefer white, anything dry with good acidity and a medium body will do nicely.

Shellfish Baked "in the Shell"

Elegant yet easy to make, this sophisticated any-season casserole can star at your next buffet. Just be sure, when making the hollandaise, to add the hot butter in a slow stream to avoid curdling the egg yolks. Assemble the dish hours ahead and let it bake while you're relaxing with your guests.

½ lb/250 g conchiglie, cooked (see page 10)

•

¾ lb/375 g small scallops
¾ lb/375 g medium prawns, peeled and deveined
2 shallots, finely minced
4 tablespoons/60 g/2 oz butter
½ cup/120 mL/4 fl oz dry white wine
Salt and finely ground white pepper to taste
1 cup/185 g/6 oz fresh or frozen peas

Tarragon Hollandaise Sauce
6 egg yolks
¼ cup/30 g/1 oz fresh tarragon leaves, coarsely chopped
¼ cup/60 mL/2 fl oz lemon juice
1 tablespoon finely minced or grated lemon zest
½ teaspoon salt, or to taste
½ teaspoon finely ground white pepper, or to taste
1 cup/250 g/8 oz butter, heated to bubbling

•

½ cup/60 g/2 oz toasted almond halves or slivers (see page 141)

Sauté scallops, prawns and shallots in butter over medium heat, stirring constantly, until they begin to change color, about 2 to 3 minutes. Add wine, raise heat to high and cook until liquid reduces by about half. Adjust seasonings; stir in peas; drain and reserve liquid.

For Tarragon Hollandaise Sauce: Process egg yolks, tarragon, lemon juice and zest, salt and pepper at low speed in a blender (liquidizer) or food processor until tarragon is finely chopped. Slowly pour in hot butter and process until mixture is smooth and slightly thickened, about 30 seconds to 1 minute.

Arrange pasta shells in a baking dish and toss with reserved scallop and prawn liquid. Toss again with about three-quarters of the sauce; top with shellfish mixture, remaining sauce and almonds. Bake, covered, in a preheated oven (400°F/200°C/gas mark 6) until heated through, about 20 minutes. Serve hot.

To Drink: With this creamy, rich sauce, a big, buttery Chardonnay would match beautifully — or try a full-flavored sparkler.

South Pacific Mahi-Mahi

Mahi-mahi, or dolphin fish, a meaty, tasty and versatile Pacific fish, stays moist and tender inside this crunchy nut crust. The sweet lychee fruit and creamy coconut milk balance the red curry sauce's fire.

¾ lb/375 g medium egg noodles

•

1 lb/500 g mahi-mahi (dolphin fish) fillets
2 egg whites, beaten
¼ cup/30 g/1 oz finely minced cashews
¼ cup/60 mL/2 fl oz peanut or other vegetable oil

Curry Sauce
1 cup/250 mL/8 fl oz Fish Stock (see page 139)
1 cup/250 mL/8 fl oz canned coconut milk**
1 to 2 tablespoons red curry paste,** or to taste
¼ cup/20 g/¾ oz grated unsweetened coconut**
¼ cup/40 g/1 oz halved fresh or canned lychees**
⅓ cup/80 mL/3 fl oz lime juice
4 green (spring) onions, thinly sliced (white plus 2 in/5 cm green)
½ cup/60 g/2 oz fresh cilantro (coriander) leaves, coarsely chopped
Salt to taste

•

Lime wedges
Cilantro (coriander) sprigs

Dip mahi-mahi in egg white, then cashews. Sauté in peanut oil over medium heat until crust is golden and fish just cooked through, about 2 to 3 minutes per side. Remove mahi-mahi and set aside.

In the same pan, combine Fish Stock, coconut milk, curry paste, coconut, lychees and lime juice and simmer 10 to 15 minutes. Stir in green onions and cilantro and adjust seasonings.

Meanwhile, cook noodles (see page 10) about 8 minutes. Toss with half the sauce; top with mahi-mahi and remaining sauce. Serve hot.

To Drink: Try a medium-weight beer or fruity, slightly sweet white such as a Gewürztraminer — or a rich, toasty sparkler to pick up these nutty flavors.

**Available in Asian groceries or some supermarkets

Curried Shellfish

This medium-hot curry, vaguely Indian in inspiration, makes a wonderful do-ahead addition to a buffet or potluck. You can make the sauce beforehand and freeze it, or assemble the entire dish up to a day in advance and bake it just before serving.

½ lb/250 g elbow macaroni

∎

1 dozen medium clams (about 1 lb/500g)
½ cup/120 mL/4 fl oz water
About 1 cup/250 mL/8 fl oz Fish Stock (see page 139)
1 medium onion, finely chopped
2 tablespoons curry powder
2 tablespoons vegetable oil
2 cloves garlic
1 cup canned coconut milk**
2 tablespoons lime juice
1 tablespoon fresh ginger juice (see page 140)
1 lb/500 g medium prawns, peeled and deveined
1 crab (2 lb/1 kg), cooked, cleaned and cracked (see page 14)
½ cup/120 mL/4 fl oz plain yogurt
Salt to taste

Cook the macaroni (see page 10) about 10 minutes.

Meanwhile, steam clams with water until they open, about 5 minutes. Strain and measure liquid. Add enough Fish Stock to total 2 cups/500 mL/16 fl oz and set aside.

Sauté onion and curry powder in vegetable oil over medium heat until soft and translucent, about 5 to 7 minutes. When onions are almost done, stir in garlic and sauté until soft and fragrant. Stir in coconut milk, lime juice and ginger juice; simmer 10 minutes.

Stir in prawns and simmer until just cooked through, about 2 to 3 minutes. Add crab, clams and yogurt; heat through and adjust seasonings.

Pour mixture over elbow macaroni in an ovenproof dish. Cover and bake in a preheated oven (375°F/190°C/gas mark 5) until heated through, 15 to 20 minutes. Serve hot.

To Drink: A light, fruity or slightly sweet white wine would do nicely — but for a party mood, break out the champagne flutes and uncork the bubbly.

** Available in Asian groceries or some supermarkets

Vietnamese Garlic-Pepper Prawns

Considering that Vietnam spent many years under French dominion, this East-West hybrid, with its liberal dose of butter and wine, comes about quite naturally. The Asian influence, too, is unmistakable here, making for a happy fusion of two worlds. Make sure to cook the noodles very briefly so they don't turn to mush.

1 lb/500 g fresh thin Chinese-style noodles**

Marinade
2 tablespoons lemon juice
2 tablespoons vegetable oil
2 tablespoons fresh ginger juice (see page 140)
½ cup/60 g/2 oz fresh cilantro (coriander) leaves, finely chopped
2 green (spring) onions, thinly sliced (white plus 2 in/5 cm green)
•
1½ lb/750 g medium prawns, peeled and deveined
¼ lb/120 g clarified butter (see page 140)
8 to 12 medium cloves garlic, finely minced, or to taste
1 cup/250 mL/8 fl oz dry white wine
½ tablespoon freshly ground black pepper
Salt to taste
•
Lemon wedges
Cilantro (coriander) sprigs
1 green (spring) onion, thinly sliced (white plus 2 in/5 cm green)

Combine ingredients for marinade and marinate prawns in the refrigerator for 1 hour. Sauté marinated prawns in butter over medium-high heat until they just begin to change color, about 2 to 3 minutes. Remove prawns and set aside. Stir in garlic and cook, stirring, until fragrant and slightly softened, about 2 to 3 minutes. Add wine and pepper; cook until liquid reduces by about half. Return prawns to pan and cook 1 to 2 minutes to blend flavors. Adjust seasonings.

Cook the noodles (see page 10) about 2 minutes and toss with about three-quarters of the sauce. Top with prawns and remaining sauce. Garnish with lemon, cilantro and green onion and serve hot.

To Drink: You can either match the rich flavors of this dish with a big, buttery Chardonnay or contrast them with a high-acid wine such as a Sauvignon Blanc. Or get the best of both with a full-flavored yet tart sparkling wine.

**Available in Asian groceries or some supermarkets

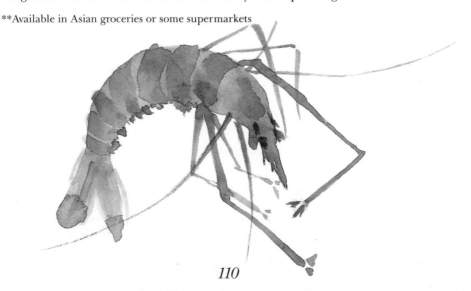

Pan-Seared Trout in Black Bean Sauce

Inspired by classic Chinese black bean sauce preparations, this easy but impressive combo substitutes rice-shaped riso or orzo pasta for the usual steamed rice. You can find black beans packed in glass jars, often flavored with garlic or spices. Salty and strong-flavored, they take some getting used to, but as with all acquired tastes, they're addictive.

½ lb/250 g riso or orzo

•

4 small or 2 large trout (2 lb/1 kg in all), preferably boneless
½ tablespoon soy sauce
1 tablespoon sesame oil**

Black Bean Sauce
½ cup/120 mL/4 fl oz Fish Stock (see page 139)
½ cup/60 g/2 oz black beans,** with their liquid
4 cloves garlic, finely minced
1 tablespoon sesame oil**
2 green (spring) onions, thinly sliced (white plus 2 in/5 cm green)
2 tablespoons finely minced or grated orange zest
2 tablespoons fresh ginger juice (see page 140)
½ cup/60 g/2 oz fresh cilantro (coriander) leaves, coarsely chopped
1 tablespoon chili sauce,** or to taste
½ teaspoon five-spice powder**

•

Lemon wedges
Cilantro (coriander) sprigs

Rub trout with soy sauce and sauté in sesame oil over medium heat, until cooked through, about 3 to 5 minutes or more per side, depending on size. Remove trout and set aside.

Cook the riso (see page 10) about 8 minutes.

Meanwhile, in the same pan as you cooked the trout, sauté garlic in sesame oil over low-medium heat until soft and fragrant, about 5 to 7 minutes. Stir in remaining sauce ingredients and simmer 5 minutes to blend flavors.

Toss pasta with three-quarters of the sauce on a platter. Top with trout and remaining sauce. Garnish with lemon and cilantro and serve hot.

To Drink: This hearty sauce can handle a light-to-medium-bodied red or a full-flavored beer as well as a sweet, fruity white or sparkling wine.

**Available at Asian groceries and some supermarkets

Szechwan Noodles with Opakapaka

The beginnings of this recipe came from the talented Barbara Tropp, a China scholar turned cookbook author and San Francisco restaurateur. Among the ingredients I've added, the five-spice powder, for instance, lends an exotic sweet-spicy flavor. (Contrary to its name, this Chinese staple can contain more than five spices, often including cinnamon, clove, star anise, licorice root, ginger, Szechwan peppercorns and fennel or anise seed.) The opakapaka, a tender, white-fleshed Hawaiian fish, makes this a well-rounded cold entree, but feel free to substitute another white fish or cooked shrimp or crabmeat.

2 lb/1 kg fresh thin Chinese-style egg noodles,** cooked (see page 10)

■

1 lb/500 g opakapaka fillet or other mild white fish
½ tablespoon sesame oil**
½ tablespoon soy sauce
1 teaspoon five-spice powder**

Szechwan Dressing
¼ cup/60 mL/2 fl oz sesame oil**
¼ cup/60 mL/2 fl oz black soy sauce**
¼ cup/60 mL/2 fl oz Chinese black vinegar** or balsamic vinegar
1 to 2 tablespoons chili oil,** or to taste
4 to 6 cloves garlic, finely minced
2 tablespoons fresh ginger juice (see page 140)
1 tablespoon sugar
2 teaspoons salt

■

¼ lb/120 g snow peas (mange tout), cut into diagonal slices (½ in/1.5 cm)
1 cup/185 g/6 oz fresh or frozen corn, cooked
½ cup/60 g/2 oz fresh cilantro (coriander) leaves, coarsely chopped
2 medium carrots, grated
4 green (spring) onions, thinly sliced (white plus 2 in/5 cm green)

Rub opakapaka with sesame oil and soy sauce and coat evenly with five-spice powder. Grill, barbecue or broil until just cooked through, about 2 to 3 minutes per side. Chill and flake or cut into slices (½ in/1.5 cm).

Combine all ingredients for dressing and adjust seasonings. Toss noodles with dressing and remaining ingredients and top with opakapaka. Serve chilled.

To Drink: A light, fruity or slightly sweet white or sparkling wine, or a good frosty beer, will balance the heat of the spices.

**Available in Asian groceries and some supermarkets

Rice Noodles with Swordfish Satay

These Indonesian-style fish kabobs, marinated in a gingery peanut sauce and then grilled on the barbeque, take on a rich, intense flavor. Cook the marinade down to make a thick satay sauce, which dresses both the skewers of fish and their bed of tender-chewy rice noodles.

½ lb/250 g thin dried rice noodles,** soaked (see page 10)

Peanut Marinade
1 cup/250 mL/8 fl oz canned coconut milk**
½ cup/60 g/2 oz unsalted roasted peanuts
¼ cup/60 mL/2 fl oz lime juice
¼ cup/60 mL/2 fl oz Shaohsing rice wine** or dry sherry
2 green (spring) onions, thinly sliced (white plus 2 in/5 cm green)
4 cloves garlic, finely minced
2 tablespoons dark soy sauce**
1 tablespoon fresh ginger juice (see page 140)
1 teaspoon chili oil**
•
1 lb/500 g swordfish, halibut or shark, cut into cubes (1½ in/4 cm)
•
Cilantro (coriander) sprigs

Combine ingredients for Peanut Marinade in a blender (liquidizer) or food processor and puree until smooth. Marinate fish at least 1 hour in refrigerator. Remove fish from marinade and thread on wooden or metal skewers.

Cook Peanut Marinade over medium heat for 5 to 8 minutes, until slightly thickened. Grill, barbecue or broil fish, turning once, until barely cooked through, about 1 to 2 minutes per side. Add fish juices to the peanut sauce.

Drain the rice noodles well and toss with sauce. Transfer to a serving platter or individual plates and arrange fish on top. Garnish with cilantro and serve warm.

To Drink: This rich, full-flavored dish, with dense-fleshed broiled fish, can handle a light- to medium-bodied red wine, as well as fruity whites and sparklers.

**Available in Asian groceries or some supermarkets

*Seared Ahi with Wasabi-Ginger Beurre Rouge

This East-West winner fuses the classic French beurre rouge (red wine butter sauce) with two traditional Asian ingredients, wasabi (spicy Japanese horseradish) and ginger. The top-quality ahi tuna, sizzled in hot butter and served while still rare at the center, looks like fine beefsteak but cuts with a fork and melts in the mouth.

½ lb/250 g fresh lemon fettuccine (see page 137)
2 tablespoons/30 g/1 oz butter
¼ cup/30 g/1 oz fresh parsley leaves, coarsely chopped
Salt to taste

▪

¼ cup/60 g/2 oz butter, preferably clarified
1 lb/500 g sashimi-grade ahi tuna steak (1 in/2.5 cm thick)
½ cup/120 mL/4 fl oz dry red wine
2 tablespoons fresh ginger juice (see page 140)
½ tablespoon soy sauce
1 to 2 tablespoons powdered wasabi**
1 tablespoon lemon juice
1 teaspoon finely minced or grated lemon zest
Salt and freshly ground pepper to taste

Melt half the butter over high heat and sear tuna quickly, 30 seconds to 1 minute on each side, so that surface chars slightly and interior remains very rare. Remove fish, cut across the grain into very thin slices and set aside. Deglaze pan with wine; lower heat to medium and simmer until reduced by half. Stir in ginger, soy, wasabi, lemon juice and zest with pan off heat, stir in remaining butter, one small piece at a time. Adjust seasonings.

Meanwhile, cook the fettuccine (see page 10) about 2 minutes. Toss with butter, parsley and salt. Arrange sliced tuna over pasta and top with sauce. Serve hot.

To Drink: With the combination of meaty tuna and a red wine sauce, a light, fruity red such as a Beaujolais, Pinot Noir or light Zinfandel would be your best bet. If you opt for sparkling wine, look for a blanc de noirs.

**Available in Asian groceries or some supermarkets

Open-Face Omelet with Fusilli and Sole

This tasty combination first came about one lazy weekend when a pair of unexpected guests stayed for supper. Suddenly, fillet of sole for two would have to feed four. A quick trip to the fridge unearthed some nice fresh eggs, some leftover pasta and a few peas from the night before. Presto: instant dinner!

½ lb/250 g fusilli, cooked (see page 10)
2 tablespoons/30 g/1 oz butter
½ cup/90 g/3 oz freshly grated parmesan cheese
1 cup/185 g/6 oz cooked peas
¼ cup/30 g/1 oz fresh parsley leaves, coarsely chopped
Salt and freshly ground white or black pepper to taste
■
¾ lb/375 g sole, in 4 fillets
1 egg white, beaten
½ cup/30 g/1oz unseasoned bread crumbs
2 tablespoons olive oil
½ cup/120 mL/4 fl oz dry white wine
2 tablespoons lemon juice
Salt and freshly ground white or black pepper to taste
■
8 eggs
¼ cup/45 g/1½ oz finely minced red (Spanish) onion
Salt and freshly ground white or black pepper to taste
2 tablespoons olive oil

Cook fusilli (see page 10) about 12 minutes. Toss with butter, parmesan, peas and parsley; adjust seasonings. Set aside.

Dip sole in egg white, then in bread crumbs. Sauté in olive oil 4 minutes per side. Add wine and cook, stirring, until alcohol evaporates and liquid reduces and soaks into the fish, about 2 to 3 minutes longer. Remove from heat; stir in lemon juice and adjust seasonings.

Beat eggs with onion, salt and pepper. In a medium nonstick pan, heat ½ tablespoon olive oil over medium-high heat. Ladle one-quarter of the egg mixture into the pan, tilting pan so egg completely covers surface of pan. When completely cooked, remove omelet and repeat to make three more omelets.

Place each omelet on a plate. Top with pasta and sole and serve hot.

To Drink: The chilled Spanish cava sparkling wine we drank was excellent with the eggs, the cheesy pasta and the toasty breaded fish — but just about any easy-drinking white wine or bubbly would do.

Basque Baked Merluza

The Basque region of Spain, which stretches from the Pyrenees to the Bay of Biscay, boasts a unique language, a varied cuisine rich in seafood and fresh vegetables. In this recipe, I've added pasta to a typical Basque seafood dish whose main ingredient, whiting (merluza), has the advantage of a very low price tag. Some languages are indeed universal.

½ lb/250 g fusilli

•

2 medium onions, finely chopped
½ cup/120 mL/4 fl oz olive oil
4 to 6 cloves garlic, finely chopped
1 medium yellow or red bell pepper (capsicum), cut into thin strips
1 to 2 small fresh hot red chiles, finely minced (optional)
½ lb/250 g string (French green) beans, halved
1 cup/250 g/8 oz fresh or canned tomatoes, coarsely chopped
1 cup/250 mL/8 fl oz dry white wine
½ cup/60 g/2 oz fresh parsley leaves, coarsely chopped, divided
Salt and freshly ground pepper to taste
1½ lb/750 g medium whiting, cleaned, heads and tails removed (or use fillets)

Cook the fusilli (see page 10) about 12 minutes.

Meanwhile, sauté onions in olive oil over medium heat until soft and translucent, about 5 to 7 minutes. When onions are almost done, stir in garlic, bell pepper and chile and sauté until garlic is soft and fragrant. Stir in string beans, tomatoes and wine and simmer 10 minutes. Add half the parsley and adjust seasonings.

If using whole whiting, fillet fish and discard bones. Place cooked fusilli in a large casserole or baking pan. Toss with about three-quarters of the sauce; top with whiting and remaining sauce. Bake, covered, in a preheated oven (400°F/200°C/gas mark 6) for 40 minutes, until whiting and string beans are tender. Garnish with remaining parsley and serve hot.

To Drink: Simple, rustic foods call for simple, rustic wines — even a good jug white, served in tumblers, will flatter a homey dish such as this.

Prawns and Feta on Pepper Pappardelle

The cool, lively flavors of this easy, rustic, Greek-inspired dish make it a natural for summer entertaining, indoors or out. If you feel like firing up the barbecue, you can add even more flavor to the shrimp by grilling rather than sautéing them. Just toss them in a little olive oil first so they'll stay moist. Either way, you'll have to break open their shells by hand, so be sure to supply extra napkins. And by all means — suck on the shells and lick your fingers to get every last drop!

1 lb/500 g fresh black-pepper pappardelle cooked, (see page 137)
2 tablespoons extra-virgin olive oil
Salt to taste

■

1 lb/500 g medium prawns
¼ cup/60 mL/2 fl oz olive oil
1 cup/250 mL/8 fl oz dry white wine
2 tablespoons lemon juice
½ cup/90 g/3 oz finely chopped red (Spanish) onion
¼ cup/20 g/¾ oz Greek olives, pitted and quartered lengthwise
¼ cup/30 g/1 oz fresh parsley leaves, coarsely chopped
2 tablespoons fresh mint leaves, finely minced
2 to 4 cloves garlic (or more to taste), finely minced
Salt and freshly ground black or white pepper to taste

■

½ lb/250 g feta cheese, cut into cubes (½ in/2.5 cm)
Lemon wedges
Parsley and mint sprigs

Toss freshly drained pappardelle with olive oil and salt and cool to room temperature.

With scissors or a sharp knife, slit each prawn shell along the back and remove vein without removing shell. Sauté prawns over medium-high heat in olive oil, stirring often, until just cooked through, about 2 to 3 minutes. Remove prawns and set aside. Add white wine to pan and cook, stirring constantly, until reduced by about half. Remove from heat and stir in lemon juice, red onion, olives, parsley, mint, garlic and reserved prawns. Adjust seasonings and cool sauce to room temperature.

Toss pasta with about three-quarters of the sauce and place onto a wide serving platter. Arrange prawns and feta over pasta and top with remaining sauce. Garnish with lemon, parsley and mint. Serve at room temperature.

To Drink: The full-flavored wines of Greece have evolved with the country's robust, herb-laced cuisine. If you haven't acquired a taste for the pine-scented Retsina, try to find an unresinated Greek white instead. You won't go wrong with a dry Italian or California white, either.

Spaghetti with Grilled Prawns and Spiced Baba Ganoush

Eggplant, or aubergine, treasured throughout the Mediterranean, truly comes into its own in the ubiquitous Middle Eastern spread known as baba ganoush. This version includes caramelized onions and garlic, which add rich sweetness and depth of flavor.

1 lb/500 g spaghetti

•

1 lb/500 g medium prawns, shelled and deveined
¼ cup/60 mL/2 fl oz olive oil
¼ cup/60 mL/2 fl oz dry white wine
2 tablespoons lemon juice

Baba Ganoush
2 medium or 3 small eggplants (aubergines), about 2 lb/1 kg
2 medium onions
1 medium bulb garlic
½ cup/120 mL/4 fl oz olive oil
½ cup/120 mL/4 fl oz yogurt
½ cup/60 g/2 oz fresh cilantro (coriander) leaves
2 tablespoons pine nuts (kernels) or walnuts
2 tablespoons lemon juice
½ tablespoon finely minced or grated lemon zest
½ tablespoon ground cumin
¼ to ½ teaspoon cayenne (optional)
Salt and freshly ground pepper to taste

•

Cilantro (coriander) sprigs

Marinate prawns with olive oil, wine and lemon juice for 1 to 2 hours in the refrigerator.

For Baba Ganoush: Cut eggplants and onions in half lengthwise; cut whole garlic bulb in half crosswise. Coat cut surfaces lightly with some of the olive oil. Place eggplants and onions, cut side down, in a baking pan. Wrap garlic in foil and add to pan. Bake vegetables in an oven preheated 400°F/200°C/gas mark 6 until very soft, about 45 minutes to 1 hour. Cool slightly, scoop the softened eggplant and onion pulp out of skins and chop coarsely. Squeeze out softened garlic and add to mixture. Place vegetables in a blender or food processor, add remaining ingredients for Baba Ganoush and puree. Adjust seasonings.

Cook spaghetti (see page 10) about 10 minutes.

Thread prawns on skewers and grill, barbecue or broil, turning once, until just cooked through, about 1 to 2 minutes per side. Cool slightly and remove from skewers.

Toss spaghetti with about three-quarters of the Baba Ganoush; top with prawns and remaining sauce. Garnish with cilantro sprigs and serve slightly warm, slightly chilled or at room temperature.

To Drink: Serve a fruity or slightly sweet white or sparkling wine, or a light-bodied red, preferably chilled.

Perch Paprikash

This classic paprikash preparation teams tender freshwater perch with tomato, sour cream and sweet paprika, the ubiquitous Hungarian mainstay. Serve the creamy, rosy-pink combination on a bed of homey egg noodles.

½ lb/250 g egg noodles
2 tablespoons/30 g/1 oz butter
Salt to taste

·

1 medium onion, finely chopped
2 tablespoons/30 g/1 oz butter
2 cloves garlic, finely minced
1 medium red bell pepper (capsicum), diced
2 tablespoons good-quality Hungarian sweet ground paprika
½ cup/120 g/4 oz finely chopped fresh or canned tomato
1 cup/250 mL/8 fl oz Fish Stock (see page 139) or vegetable stock
1¼ lb/620 g freshwater perch or other white fish fillet,
cut into slices (1 in/2.5 cm)
½ cup/120 mL/4 fl oz sour cream (crème fraîche)
¼ cup/30 g/1 oz fresh parsley leaves, coarsely chopped
Salt and freshly ground white or black pepper to taste

Sauté onion in butter over medium heat until soft and translucent, about 5 to 7 minutes.

Cook noodles (see page 10) about 8 minutes. Meanwhile, when onions are almost done, stir in garlic, red bell pepper and paprika and sauté until garlic is slightly softened and fragrant. Stir in tomato; cover and cook 5 minutes. Add stock and heat through. Add fish and simmer until barely cooked through, about 2 to 3 minutes. Stir in sour cream and parsley and heat through. Adjust seasonings.

Toss noodles with butter and salt and arrange on a serving platter. Toss with about three-quarters of the sauce; arrange fish over pasta and top with remaining sauce. Serve hot.

To Drink: A fruity white or light red will do nicely, but for a startling color match, try a salmon-pink blanc de noirs sparkling wine.

Greek Baked Prawns

In this easy, make-ahead casserole, capers and feta cheese add a delightful salty tang to the shrimp and the curly, corkscrew-shaped pasta. The Greek oregano, which keeps its intense flavor even when dried, adds a pleasant pungency. Notice that although the ingredients in this recipe seem quite similar to those on page 118, the results are completely different.

½ lb/250 g fusilli, cooked (see page 10)
2 tablespoons olive oil
Salt to taste

■

1½ lb/750 g medium prawns, peeled and deveined
½ cup/120 mL/4 fl oz olive oil, divided
2 medium onions, finely chopped
4 cloves garlic, finely minced
¼ cup/60 mL/2 fl oz ouzo or anisette
½ cup/120 mL/4 fl oz dry white wine
1 tablespoon lemon juice
1 cup/250 g/8 oz fresh or canned tomatoes, diced
¼ cup/30 g/1 oz fresh parsley leaves, coarsely chopped
2 tablespoons capers
½ tablespoon dried oregano, preferably Greek, plus extra for garnish
1 teaspoon freshly ground black pepper, or to taste
½ teaspoon ground cumin
¼ teaspoon cayenne, or to taste (optional), plus extra for garnish
¾ lb/375 g feta cheese (preferably Greek or Bulgarian), crumbled

Cook fusilli (see page 10) about 12 minutes. Toss with olive oil and salt and arrange in a baking dish.

Sauté prawns in half the olive oil over medium heat, stirring, until they just start to change color, about 1 to 2 minutes. Remove prawns and set aside.

Add remaining olive oil and sauté onions over medium heat until soft and translucent, about 5 to 7 minutes. When onions are almost done, stir in garlic and sauté until soft and fragrant. Add ouzo, light with a match and flambé, shaking pan until alcohol evaporates and flame goes out. Add wine and lemon juice and cook 2 to 3 minutes. Stir in remaining ingredients except feta. Return prawns to pan; stir well and adjust seasonings.

Stir half the prawn mixture into the pasta. Top with the remaining prawn mixture, feta and remaining olive oil. Dust with a little extra cayenne, if used, and dried oregano. Bake, covered, in a preheated oven (375°F/190°C/gas mark 5) until heated through, about 20 to 30 minutes. Serve hot.

To Drink: Try a Retsina or other Greek white, a Sauvignon Blanc or other dry, crisp white or sparkling wine.

Cretan Monkfish

Monkfish, also known as angler, lotte and goosefish, thrives in Mediterranean waters and graces skillets and stewpots throughout Southern Europe. A bizarre-looking fish with a jutting jaw and a long slim tail, it angles for prey by dangling a fishingpole-like antenna through the water. Where monkfish is plentiful and cheap, its sweet, dense-textured tail meat has earned it the moniker "poor man's lobster."

½ lb/250 g creste di gallo

Spiced Tomato Sauce
1 lb/500 g small white onions, peeled
12 whole medium cloves garlic, peeled
½ cup/120 mL/4 fl oz olive oil, divided
1 tablespoon whole black peppercorns
1 tablespoon whole allspice berries
2 bay leaves
1 tablespoon ground cumin
3 cups/750 g/1¼ lb coarsely chopped fresh or canned plum tomatoes
½ cup/120 mL/4 fl oz dry red wine
½ cup/120 mL/4 fl oz red wine vinegar

•

1½ lb/750 g monkfish fillet, cut into strips (1 in/2.5 cm)
2 oranges, peeled and thinly sliced

Over low heat, sauté onions and garlic cloves in half the olive oil until pale golden and slightly softened, about 8 to 10 minutes. Stir in remaining ingredients for sauce and simmer 15 minutes. (Note: If you don't want whole spices in your finished sauce, tie them in cheesecloth and remove before serving.)

Halfway through simmering, cook the creste di gallo (see page 10) about 12 minutes. Toss creste di gallo with 2 tablespoons olive oil, then with about three-quarters of the sauce, and place in a baking dish. Arrange monkfish and orange slices on top. Pour remaining sauce over fish, drizzle with remaining olive oil and bake in a preheated oven (375°F/190°C/gas mark 5) for 25 to 30 minutes, or until monkfish is tender. Serve hot.

To Drink: A fruity, slightly sweet white wine, especially something spicy like a Gewürztraminer, would match handsomely.

Moroccan Roast Sea Bass

*Ruffly lasagne noodles, roughly snapped, make a rustic bed for this spicy striped bass.
The exotic charmoula, a complex blend of spices, herbs and olive oil, reigns as one of
Morocco's culinary treasures.*

½ lb/250 g lasagne, broken into irregular pieces (2 in/5 cm)

Charmoula
1 cup/250 mL/8 fl oz olive oil
½ cup/120 mL/4 fl oz lemon juice
1 cup/120 g/4 oz fresh parsley leaves, coarsely chopped
½ cup/60 g/2 oz fresh cilantro (coriander) leaves, coarsely chopped
2 green (spring) onions, thinly sliced (white plus 2 in/5 cm green)
2 to 4 cloves garlic, finely minced
1 tablespoon sweet ground paprika
½ tablespoon ground cumin
½ to 1 teaspoon cayenne, or to taste
Salt and freshly ground pepper to taste
▪
1 small whole sea bass (about 3 lb/1.5 kg or 1½ lb/750 g) fillets

Combine all ingredients for the Charmoula. Place fish in a baking dish and
spoon about ½ cup/120 mL/4 fl oz Charmoula over it, coating all sides. Roast
fish, uncovered, in a preheated oven (425°F/210°C/gas mark 7) until cooked
through, about 30 to 40 minutes (less for fillets). If using whole fish, carefully
fillet fish after cooking, keeping whole fillets as intact as possible and removing
small bones.

About halfway through baking the fish, cook lasagne (see page 10) about 15
minutes. Toss with about three-quarters of the remaining Charmoula; top with
fish and remaining Charmoula. Serve hot.

To Drink: You can serve this dish with a white, light red or sparkling wine. The
spicier you make it, the fruitier or sweeter the wine should be.

Mahi-Mahi and Mushroom Mostaccioli

Another name for mahi-mahi, a native of warm Pacific waters, is dolphin fish (or just plain dolphin) — but don't worry, you're not eating Flipper! This dolphin is not a marine mammal but a true fish, with firm, tasty meat that can stand up to a full-flavored sauce.

½ lb/250 g mostaccioli, cooked (see page 10)

•

1 lb/500 g mahi-mahi fillet, cut into slices (½ in/1.5 cm)
¼ cup/60 mL/2 fl oz olive oil, divided
2 medium onions, finely chopped
2 tablespoons/30 g/1 oz butter
½ lb/250 g mushrooms, thinly sliced
1 cup/250 mL/8 fl oz dry red wine
½ tablespoon finely chopped fresh rosemary
½ teaspoon freshly ground black pepper, or to taste
½ cup/120 mL/4 fl oz heavy (double) cream
Salt to taste

Sauté mahi-mahi slices over medium-high heat in 2 tablespoons olive oil until just cooked through, about 1 minute per side. Remove fish and keep warm. In the same pan, sauté onions in remaining olive oil and butter over medium heat until soft and translucent, about 5 to 7 minutes. Stir in mushrooms; cover and cook, stirring occasionally, until mushrooms are tender, about 15 to 20 minutes. Add wine, rosemary and pepper; simmer, stirring, until liquid reduces by about half. Stir in cream and heat through. Adjust seasonings.

About halfway through simmering the sauce, cook mostaccioli (see page 10) about 12 minutes. Toss with about three-quarters of the mushroom sauce; top with mahi-mahi slices and remaining sauce. Serve hot.

To Drink: This meaty fish, particularly in this hearty preparation, can handle a light- to medium-bodied red wine such as a Pinot Noir or a light Merlot. If you prefer white, choose an oak-aged Chardonnay or a full-bodied sparkler.

Abalone Piccata

Freshly plucked from the ocean shallows, this seagoing snail – one of the most highly prized treasures of Neptune's domain – yields incomparably sweet meat. If you don't count any "ab" divers among your friends, buy abalone fresh or frozen, or substitute giant squid (calamari).

8 oz/250 g farfalle
2 tablespoons/30 g/1 oz butter
Salt to taste
▪
¾ lb/375 g fresh abalone, cleaned, thinly sliced and pounded
¼ cup/45 g/1½ oz all-purpose (plain) flour
Salt to taste
¼ cup/60 mL/2 fl oz olive oil
2 tablespoons/30 g/1 oz butter
2 medium shallots, finely minced
½ cup/120 mL/4 fl oz dry white wine
2 tablespoons lemon juice
½ tablespoon finely minced lemon zest
½ cup/120 mL/4 fl oz Fish Stock (see page 139)
2 tablespoons capers
¼ cup/30 g/1 oz fresh parsley leaves, coarsely chopped
Salt and freshly ground white or black pepper to taste

Cook the farfalle (see page 10) about 12 minutes.

Meanwhile, dredge abalone slices in flour and salt and sauté quickly over high heat in olive oil and butter until golden outside and just cooked through, about 30 seconds to 1 minute per side. Remove and reserve abalone. Stir in shallots and sauté, stirring often, until soft and fragrant, about 3 to 5 minutes. Add wine, lemon juice and zest; raise heat to high and cook until liquid reduces by about half. Add remaining ingredients and simmer 2 minutes. Adjust seasonings.

Toss pasta with butter and salt, then with about three-quarters of the sauce. Top with abalone slices and remaining sauce. Serve hot.

To Drink: Try a full-flavored, buttery Chardonnay to match the richness of the dish or a crisp sparkling wine to cut through it.

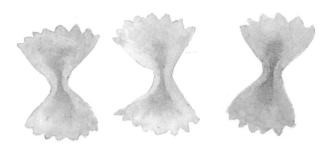

Halibut with Ziti and Olive-Rosemary Tapenade

Tapenade is a tangy Provençal specialty used either as a thick spread for bread or, thinned with olive oil, as a versatile sauce. Its earthy olive-brown color contrasts handsomely with the bright white of halibut in this rustic, casual dish.

½ lb/250 g ziti
2 tablespoons olive oil
Salt to taste

▪

1 lb/500 g halibut steak or fillet, 1 in/2.5 cm thick
1 tablespoon olive oil
½ tablespoon lemon juice

Olive-Rosemary Tapenade
1 cup/90 g/3 oz pitted Niçoise, Kalamata or other flavorful olives, coarsely chopped
½ cup/120 mL/4 fl oz extra-virgin olive oil
1 can (2 oz/60 g) anchovy fillets, drained and finely chopped
2 to 4 cloves garlic, finely minced
2 tablespoons capers, coarsely chopped
2 tablespoons lemon juice
½ cup/60 g/2 oz fresh parsley leaves, coarsely chopped
½ to 1 tablespoon finely minced fresh rosemary
Freshly ground pepper to taste

Cook ziti (see page 10) about 12 minutes. Toss with olive oil and salt.

Dip halibut in olive oil and lemon juice, coating fish evenly. Grill, barbecue or broil until just cooked through, about 2 to 3 minutes per side. Cool slightly, slice thinly and set aside.

Combine all ingredients for Olive-Rosemary Tapenade.

Toss pasta again with about three-quarters of the tapenade and arrange on a serving platter. Top with halibut slices and remaining tapenade. Serve warm, chilled or at room temperature.

To Drink: Given the bold flavors here, you'll need a full-bodied white or a rustic but not too heavy red — served in unfussy glasses.

Linguine with Clam Sauce

No pasta book — or seafood book, for that matter — would be complete without at least one recipe for this perennial favorite. This book offers two. Fresh clams, different herbs and a touch of tomato distinguish this simple version from the even easier one that follows. Try this one when you can get small, sweet-tasting clams in the shell — their fresh, briny flavor is incomparable. If not, the extra-quick version on the next page is a delicious alternative.

1 lb/500 g linguine, cooked (see page 10)

■

4 dozen small littleneck, Manila or other hardshell clams (about 3 lbs/750 g)
½ cup/120 mL/4 fl oz dry white wine
6 to 8 cloves garlic (or to taste), finely minced
¼ cup/120 mL/4 fl oz olive oil
1 cup/250 g/8 oz fresh or canned tomatoes, finely chopped
¼ cup/30 g/1 oz fresh basil leaves, coarsely chopped
¼ cup/30 g/1 oz fresh parsley leaves, coarsely chopped
2 tablespoons fresh marjoram or oregano leaves, coarsely chopped
¼ to ½ teaspoon dried hot red pepper flakes (optional)
Salt and freshly ground white or black pepper to taste

Steam clams with wine until they open, about 5 minutes. Strain and reserve liquid.

In a medium saucepan, sauté garlic in olive oil over low-medium heat, stirring often, until soft and fragrant, about 5 to 7 minutes.

Cook the linguine (see page 10) about 10 minutes.

Meanwhile, stir tomatoes and reserved clam liquid into garlic; simmer 10 minutes to blend flavors and thicken sauce slightly. Add basil, parsley, marjoram and hot pepper, if used; adjust seasonings. Stir in clams and heat through.

Toss linguine with about three-quarters of the sauce in a large serving bowl. Top with remaining sauce and clams and serve hot.

To Drink: Try a tart, full-flavored Sauvignon Blanc or Italian white, or even a delicate red such as a Beaujolais or light-bodied Zinfandel.

*Quick Linguine with Clam Sauce

Long and thin like spaghetti but flattened just slightly to help hold onto sauce, linguine, or "little tongues," are the classic shape for shellfish — especially clams. If you prefer a soupier consistency, drain the noodles quickly so that they retain more moisture.

1 lb/500 g linguine

■

6 to 8 cloves garlic (or to taste), finely minced
½ cup/120 mL/4 fl oz olive oil
1 cup/250 mL/8 fl oz dry white wine
3 cans (6 oz/185 g) chopped clams (baby clams)
¼ cup/30 g/1 oz fresh parsley leaves, coarsely chopped
2 tablespoons fresh marjoram or oregano leaves, coarsely chopped
¼ to ½ teaspoon dried hot red pepper flakes (optional)
Salt and freshly ground white or black pepper to taste

Cook the linguine (see page 10) about 10 minutes.

Meanwhile, sauté garlic in olive oil over low-medium heat, stirring often, until soft and fragrant, about 5 to 7 minutes. Add wine, raise heat to high and cook until liquid reduces by about half.

Stir in clams with their liquid, parsley, marjoram and hot pepper, if used. Lower heat to medium and bring sauce just to boiling, stirring occasionally. Adjust seasonings.

Toss linguine with about three-quarters of the sauce in a large serving bowl. Top with remaining sauce and serve hot.

To Drink: A crisp California Sauvignon Blanc, with its slightly herbal flavors, or a tangy dry Italian white such as a Soave or Verdicchio, would be ideal.

Crab-Spinach Cannelloni

This is a wonderfully elegant party dish that you can assemble in the morning or even the day before. And you'll save time and effort with the simplified cream sauce: instead of standing at the stove and stirring it constantly, you just pop the sauce in the oven to finish cooking. Start baking the cannelloni when your guests arrive, then open a bottle of bubbly and enjoy yourselves as the rich aromas fill the kitchen.

½ lb/250 g cannelloni or manicotti, cooked (see page 10)

Crab-Spinach Filling
1 medium onion, finely chopped
2 tablespoons/30 g/1 oz butter
2 tablespoons cognac or brandy
1 lb/500 g fresh crabmeat (or imitation crab)
1½ cups/230 g/8 oz cooked spinach (English spinach), finely chopped (about 1 bunch fresh or 10 oz/315 g frozen)
4 green (spring) onions, thinly sliced (white plus 2 in/5 cm green)
1 cup/120 g/4 oz ricotta or cottage cheese
¼ cup/60 mL/2 fl oz dry sherry
1 teaspoon salt
½ teaspoon freshly ground white or black pepper, or to taste

Nutmeg Cream Sauce
¼ cup/60 g/2 oz butter
¼ cup/45 g/1½ oz all-purpose (plain) flour
2 cups/500 mL/16 fl oz milk
1 teaspoon ground nutmeg
Salt and finely ground white or black pepper to taste
∎
½ cup/60 g/2 oz pistachios, shelled, skinned and coarsely chopped

Sauté onion in butter over medium heat until soft and translucent, about 5 to 7 minutes. Add cognac, light with a match and flambé, shaking pan until alcohol evaporates and flame goes out. Stir in remaining ingredients for Crab-Spinach Filling. Spoon filling into cannelloni tubes and arrange in an ovenproof pan.

For Nutmeg Cream Sauce: In an ovenproof pan, melt butter over low heat and sauté flour until it thickens slightly, about 3 to 5 minutes. Stir the milk in slowly; add nutmeg and whisk until smooth. Finish cooking the sauce in a preheated oven (350°F/180°C/gas mark 4) for 20 minutes or until thick. Stir and adjust seasonings.

Spoon cream sauce over cannelloni and sprinkle with pistachios. Cover pan and bake at 400°F/200°C/gas mark 6 for about 20 minutes. Uncover pan and continue baking until pasta is heated through and sauce is bubbling, about 10 minutes longer. Serve hot.

To Drink: This rich and festive dish shows its flavors abundantly with a really fine, buttery Chardonnay or a dry, full-flavored sparkling wine.

Sand Dabs with Tomato-Olive Salsa

Sand dabs are tiny saltwater flatfish that look like baby flounder. They're usually sold "pan-dressed" (trimmed, but with bone in), but if you'd rather not wrestle with bones, use fillets of flounder or other white flatfish instead.

½ lb/250 g creste di gallo or other medium pasta

Tomato-Olive Salsa
½ lb/250 g fresh mozzarella, cut into slivers
1 lb/500 g fresh tomatoes, finely chopped
½ cup/120 mL/4 fl oz extra-virgin olive oil
½ cup/90 g/3 oz finely chopped red (Spanish) onion
4 to 6 cloves garlic, finely minced, or to taste
¼ cup/20 g/¾ oz black olives, pitted and quartered
¼ cup/20 g/¾ oz green olives, pitted and quartered
¼ cup/60 mL/2 fl oz lemon juice
1 tablespoon finely minced or grated lemon zest
¼ cup/30 g/1 oz fresh parsley leaves, coarsely choppped
¼ cup/30 g/1 oz fresh basil leaves, coarsely chopped
2 tablespoons fresh lemon thyme leaves
Salt and freshly ground black pepper to taste

▪

½ cup/30 g/1 oz seasoned bread crumbs
1 teaspoon dried oregano, crumbled
¼ teaspoon salt, or to taste
1 lb/500 g pan-dressed sand dabs or boneless white flatfish fillets
2 egg whites, beaten
¼ cup/60 mL/2 fl oz olive oil

Combine ingredients for Tomato-Olive Salsa and let stand at room temperature at least 30 minutes.

Cook creste di gallo (see page 10) about 12 minutes.

Meanwhile, combine bread crumbs, oregano and salt. Dip sand dabs in egg whites, then in bread crumb mixture. Sauté over medium heat in olive oil until just cooked through, about 3 to 4 minutes per side.

Toss pasta with about three-quarters of the salsa; top with sand dabs and remaining salsa. Serve warm or at room temperature.

To Drink: Any dry, medium-bodied white with good acidity should work well — a slightly herbal Sauvignon Blanc would be ideal.

Rockfish in Cinnamon-Tomato Sauce

This deceptively simple dish, Middle Eastern in its inspiration, gets plenty of natural sweetness from the caramelized onions and dried apricots. Spice it up or down as much as you like.

1 lb/500 g fresh fettuccine (see page 137)

·

3 medium red (Spanish) onions, thinly sliced
¼ cup/60 mL/2 fl oz olive oil
6 cloves garlic, finely minced
2 cups/500 g/1 lb finely chopped fresh or canned tomatoes
2 cups/500 mL/16 fl oz Fish Stock (see page 139)
¼ cup/45 g/1½ oz dried apricots, coarsely chopped
1 teaspoon cinnamon
½ teaspoon cayenne (optional)
1 lb/500 g red snapper, rock cod or other rockfish, cut into strips (1½ in/4 cm)
¼ cup fresh parsley leaves, coarsely chopped
Salt and freshly ground pepper to taste

Sauté onions in olive oil over low-medium heat, stirring often, until soft and translucent, about 10 to 15 minutes. When onions are almost done, stir in garlic and sauté until soft and fragrant. Stir in tomatoes, stock, apricots, cinnamon and cayenne and simmer 20 minutes. Stir in rockfish and simmer until just cooked through, about 2 to 3 minutes. Add parsley and adjust seasonings.

   Cook fettuccine (see page 10) about 2 minutes. Toss with half the sauce and arrange on a serving platter. Spoon fish over pasta and top with remaining sauce. Serve hot.

To Drink: A fruity or slightly sweet white or sparkling wine balances the heat.

Prawns Bagna Cauda

Bagna cauda (or caoda) means "hot bath" in the Piemontese dialect of northern Italy. Tradi-tionally, diners dip raw vegetables, fondue style, into a pot of bubbling nutty-sweet garlic oil, soaking up the tasty dribbles with morsels of bread. In my deluxe version, delicate vermicelli noodles substitute for the bread, and prawns add extra richness.

1 lb/500 g vermicelli
3 to 4 tablespoons olive oil
¼ cup/30 g/1 oz fresh parsley leaves, coarsely chopped
Salt to taste

Bagna Cauda Sauce
1 cup/90 g/3 oz small whole garlic cloves, peeled
1 cup/250 mL/8 fl oz olive oil
1 cup/250 g/8 oz butter, preferably clarified (see page 140)
1 can (2 oz/60 g) anchovy fillets, drained and finely chopped
¼ cup/30 g/1 oz fresh parsley leaves, coarsely chopped

•

3 lb/750 g raw vegetables (e.g. broccoli florets, cauliflower florets, string (French green) beans, button mushrooms, cherry tomatoes, green (spring) onions, red cabbage, radishes, zucchini (courgettes), red and yellow bell pepper (capsicum), carrots), washed and cut into bite-sized pieces

•

1¼ lb/620 g medium prawns, peeled and deveined
2 tablespoons olive oil
1 tablespoon lemon juice
Salt to taste

For Bagna Cauda Sauce: Simmer garlic in olive oil and butter over very low heat (an electric fondue pot is ideal) until garlic becomes very soft and golden, about 1½ to 2 hours. Stir in anchovies and parsley and keep warm at table.

Arrange vegetables attractively on a serving tray.

Cook vermicelli (see page 10) about 5 minutes. Toss with olive oil, parsley and salt. Keep warm in a chafing dish.

Sauté prawns in olive oil over medium-high heat, stirring constantly, until just cooked through, about 2 minutes. Toss with lemon juice and salt and transfer to a small serving bowl.

Serve each diner a small portion of pasta, twirled into a "nest." Everyone dips prawns and raw vegetables into the Bagna Cauda, dripping any excess on the pasta, then eating the pasta when it has absorbed enough sauce.

To Drink: You can match the richness of the Bagna Cauda and prawns with a big, buttery Chardonnay or contrast it with a tart Sauvignon Blanc or Italian white — or better yet, pop the cork on a good-quality sparkling wine.

Pappardelle with Swordfish, Tomatoes and Onions

Swordfish, a dense-fleshed, deep-water denizen, takes extremely well to the barbecue, grill or broiler. Here its rich flavor and firm texture stand up handsomely to the sweet onions lashed with dark, woodsy balsamic vinegar, the garlic-laced chunks of tomato, and the pungent fresh sage. Wide, rough-cut pappardelle noodles add to the sense of good, hearty eating. If you can't find them, just cook up some lasagne noodles and slice them irregularly.

1 lb/500 g fresh pappardelle (see page 137)
2 tablespoons extra-virgin olive oil
Salt to taste

Marinade
¼ cup/60 g/2 fl oz olive oil
2 tablespoons balsamic vinegar
24 small fresh sage leaves (or 12 large leaves, halved)
2 garlic cloves, finely minced

1 lb swordfish, cut into cubes (1½ in/4 cm)

Balsamic Onions
4 medium onions, skins on, sliced (1 in/2.5 cm)
¼ cup/60 mL/2 fl oz olive oil
2 tablespoons balsamic vinegar
Salt and freshly ground black or white pepper to taste

Sauce
2 lb/1 kg tomatoes, diced
4 cloves garlic, finely minced
½ medium red (Spanish) onion, finely chopped
12 small fresh sage leaves, thinly sliced
¼ cup/60 mL/2 f l oz extra-virgin olive oil
2 tablespoons balsamic vinegar
Salt and freshly ground pepper to taste

Combine marinade ingredients, stirring to bruise sage leaves. Marinate swordfish cubes for at least 1 hour. Thread cubes on skewers, alternating with sage leaves. Grill, barbecue or broil swordfish until slightly charred on the outside and just cooked through, about 2 to 3 minutes per side. Transfer swordfish to a cutting board, discarding sage leaves; slice thinly and set aside.

Arrange onions on a platter. Combine olive oil, balsamic vinegar, salt and pepper and spoon over onions, coating evenly. Turn onions once so that all cut surfaces absorb dressing. Grill onion slices at edges of the barbecue or further from the broiler flame or element, turning them as they char and soften. When fully cooked, transfer onions to cutting board, peel and discard skin, chop coarsely and reserve.

Combine sauce ingredients. Stir in grilled onions and adjust seasonings.

Cook pappardelle (see page 10) about 2 minutes. Toss with olive oil and salt and allow to cool slightly. Toss again with about three-quarters of the sauce, then top with swordfish and remaining sauce. Serve at room temperature.

To Drink: Try a Pinot Noir with smoky flavors to echo the fish, a Chianti, a Spanish red or a medium-weight Zinfandel. Or choose a very full-flavored white, such as a barrel-aged Chardonnay or Sauvignon Blanc.

Seared Ahi and Four-Mushroom Sauce

Forget "chicken of the sea" – FRESH tuna, when cooked au poivre and served with heaps of mushrooms and a thick, creamy sauce, tastes uncannily like fine steak. The secret is to sauté it very quickly over high heat to sear the outside while keeping the center red-rare and juicy. The green-and-white bed of "straw and hay" pasta adds a subtle color accent.

½ lb/250 g fresh egg fettuccine, preferably homemade (see page 137)
½ lb fresh spinach fettuccine, preferably homemade (see page 137)

■

1 oz/30 g dried porcini mushrooms
½ cup/120 mL/4 fl oz boiling water
1 teaspoon coarsely ground black pepper
1 lb/500 g ahi tuna steak (1 in/2.5 cm)
½ tablespoon olive oil
¾ cup/185 mL/6 fl oz red wine
2 medium red (Spanish) onions, coarsely chopped
¼ cup/60 ml/2 fl oz olive oil
2 tablespoons/30 g/1 oz butter
6 oz/185 g button mushrooms, sliced ¼ in/.5 cm thick
6 oz/185 g fresh porcini or portobello mushrooms, diced
6 oz fresh shiitake mushrooms, sliced ¼ in/.5 cm thick
½ cup/120 mL/4 fl oz half-and-half (half milk, half cream)
½ cup/120 mL/4 fl oz Fish Stock (see page 139)
⅓ lb/155 g mushroom brie, rind discarded, chopped
2 tablespoons thinly sliced fresh sage leaves
Salt to taste

■

Sage sprigs

Soak dried porcini mushrooms in boiling water until softened, about 20 to 30 minutes. Drain and reserve liquid; mince porcini finely.

Press coarsely ground pepper into both sides of fish with the heel of your hand. Heat olive oil over high heat and sear fish quickly, 30 seconds to 1 minute on each side, so that surface chars slightly but the interior remains very rare. Remove tuna and cool slightly.

Deglaze pan with wine, lower heat to medium and simmer until reduced by about half. Stir in onions, olive oil and butter and cook until onions just begin to soften, about 2 to 3 minutes. Add fresh mushrooms; cover and cook, stirring frequently, until mushrooms are tender but still slightly firm, about 6 to 8 minutes. Stir in minced porcini mushrooms and their liquid, half-and-half and Fish Stock. Heat sauce to simmering.

Cook both types of fettuccine (see page 10) about 2 minutes.

Immediately before serving, add mushroom brie and sage leaves to sauce; stir until brie melts. Adjust seasonings. Toss pasta with about three-quarters of the mushroom sauce on a large serving platter. Slice tuna diagonally across the grain in very thin slices and arrange over pasta. Top with remaining sauce. Garnish with sage sprigs and serve hot.

To Drink: With a red-meated fish, and with mushrooms and red wine in the sauce, this dish shows best alongside a not-too-tannic red wine such as a Pinot Noir or a light Merlot. A dry sparkling blanc de noirs, which is made from red grapes, is a fine option when the occasion calls for bubbly.

*Tagliarine with Scallops and Hazel-Basil Pesto

In late summer, when basil is at its flavor peak, I always take advantage of its abundance in the garden and marketplace. By blending handfuls of the fresh, fragrant leaves in the food processor with olive oil, and pouring concentrated paste into small containers, I can fill a good-sized corner of my freezer with my favorite herb. Then I'm always ready, even in midwinter, to add garlic, nuts and cheese when the urge for pesto strikes!

1 lb/500 g fresh tagliarine (see page 10)

■

¾ lb/375 g small sweet scallops
2 tablespoons olive oil
½ cup/120 mL/4 fl oz dry white wine
2 tablespoons lemon juice
Salt and freshly ground white or black pepper to taste

Hazel-Basil Pesto
¼ cup/30 g/1 oz hazelnuts, toasted (see page 141)
2 cups/250 g/8 oz fresh basil leaves
3 to 6 cloves garlic, or to taste
¼ cup/60 mL/2 fl oz olive oil
Salt and freshly ground white or black pepper to taste

Sauté scallops in olive oil over medium-high heat, stirring frequently, until they start to turn white, about 1 to 2 minutes. Add the wine and cook, stirring, until alcohol evaporates and liquid reduces slightly, about 2 to 3 minutes longer. Stir in lemon juice; adjust seasonings. Remove from heat and allow to cool slightly.

Combine ingredients for Hazel-Basil Pesto in a blender (liquidizer) or food processor until smooth. Stir pesto into scallop mixture. Adjust seasonings.

Cook the tagliarine (see page 10) about 2 minutes and toss with about three-quarters of the sauce; top with scallops and remaining sauce and serve hot.

To Drink: Because the scallops and hazelnuts are so rich, this dish can handle a medium-bodied Chardonnay or a big, full-flavored Sauvignon Blanc.

THE BASICS

Semolina Pasta

Semolina flour, made from hard durum wheat, is tastier than regular flour, has more protein and holds up better in cooking. All semolina doughs are, however, almost impossible to knead properly by hand. So this recipe combines semolina with regular flour for the best of both worlds. This pasta may be used as is, or see the next page for some flavorful variations. Pasta machines make fast work of rolling the dough, turning out uniform, even-textured sheets. (I prefer the next-to-last setting for most noodles, but I keep fettuccine one notch thicker.) Makes about 1 pound/500 g.

1 cup/155 g/5 oz fine semolina flour
2 cups/310 g/10 oz all-purpose (plain) flour
½ teaspoon salt
About 1 cup/250 mL/8 fl oz warm water

Combine the flours and salt in a food processor. With the processor running, add the water slowly through the feed tube. When the dough pulls together into a solid mass, stop adding water. Process for 2 or 3 minutes longer.

Transfer the dough to your work surface and continue kneading, pushing down on the dough with the heel of your hand as you turn it, for at least 5 minutes. Cover the dough with a towel or bowl and allow to rest for at least 10 minutes.

Slice the dough into 5 pieces. With a rolling pin, roll each piece out to the desired thinness, folding the sheet over frequently and dusting it with semolina flour as you go to keep it from sticking. Or use a pasta machine.

Fold each sheet horizontally in thirds and cut this roll of pasta into slices as wide as you want your noodles to be. Gently unfold each slice to make a noodle, sprinkling it with a little semolina flour if it seems sticky.

Cook immediately, refrigerate for up to a week or freeze for up to 3 months. Or drape the noodles over a wooden dowel until dry and store for later use.

Egg Pasta

This traditional method gives you a literally hands-on feel for the pasta right from the start.
But if saving time is important to you, use a food processor to blend the flour and eggs.
Again, consider the variations below for an even more flavorful pasta.
Makes about 1 pound/500 g.

About 3 cups/460 g/15 oz all-purpose (plain) flour
3 large eggs

On your work surface or in a large bowl, mound 2 ¼ cups/350 g/11 oz of the flour and form a well in the center. Break the eggs into the well and beat with a fork or your fingers. Using your hands, gradually stir the flour into the eggs until all the flour is incorporated. If the dough seems sticky, work in more flour.

Knead the dough, allow it to rest, divide it, roll it out and cut it to the desired width as described in the preceding Semolina Pasta recipe.

Variations

Add the following to the flour. For moist ingredients such as spinach, beets or tomato paste, you may need to add extra flour or the dough will be sticky.

Beet: 1 small beet (about ⅓ lb/165 g), boiled or baked in foil until tender, peeled and pureed or very finely chopped

Bell Pepper (Capsicum): about ½ cup/90 g/3 oz roasted red or yellow bell peppers (capsicums), see page 140

Black Pepper: about 1 tablespoon freshly ground black pepper

Citrus: about 2 tablespoons grated lemon or other citrus zest

Herb: about 2 tablespoons very finely minced strong-flavored herbs, such as rosemary, sage, marjoram or oregano

Lemon-Pepper: about 2 tablespoons of grated lemon zest and about 1 tablespoon freshly ground black pepper

Saffron: ¼ teaspoon powdered saffron

Spinach: 1 lb/500 g fresh spinach (English spinach) leaves or 1 package (10 oz/300 g) frozen spinach, cooked without added water, squeezed dry and pureed or very finely chopped

Sun-Dried Tomato: ¾ cup/60 g/2 oz oil-packed sun-dried tomatoes, drained and pureed or very finely chopped

Tomato: about 3 tablespoons tomato paste (puree)

Fish Stock

A good, rich fish stock is indispensable for many recipes in this book. Fortunately, it's very easy to make. Fish markets will often give away bones, heads and other trimmings, or sell them at a nominal price. I also save prawn, lobster and crab shells in the freezer for my stock-making. Add some aromatic vegetables, a healthy splash of wine, and you've got the makings of a beautiful broth. Cook it up in a big batch, let it cool and then freeze it in small containers. It will keep for up to 3 months in the freezer or several days in the refrigerator.
Makes about 3 quarts/3 L.

5 pounds/2.5 kg fish trimmings
10 cups/2.5 L/80 fl oz water
5 cups/1.25 L/40 fl oz dry white wine
2 carrots, coarsely chopped
2 stalks celery, with leaves, coarsely chopped
½ medium onion, coarsely chopped
4 parsley sprigs (optional)
4 garlic cloves (optional)
½ tablespoons black peppercorns (optional)

Combine all ingredients in a large stockpot over medium-high heat and bring to a boil. Simmer 30 minutes, skimming off any foam and fat and stirring occasionally. Strain and reserve liquid, discarding solids.

Mayonnaise

With the help of a food processor, homemade mayonnaise is really a breeze. Its fresh flavor is far superior to that of any commercial product; but if raw egg yolks concern you, by all means, use a good store-bought brand instead.

2 egg yolks
2 tablespoons lemon juice
1 tablespoon Dijon-style prepared mustard
½ teaspoon salt, or to taste
About 1 cup/250 mL/8 fl oz olive oil

Combine egg yolks, lemon juice, mustard and salt in a blender (liquidizer) or food processor and blend briefly. With the machine running, slowly add the oil in a very thin stream until it is incorporated and the mixture thick and glossy. Adjust seasonings.

Roasted Bell Peppers

Bell peppers, or capsicums, of any color develop an incomparably delicious, sweet flavor when roasted. Even staunch bell-pepper haters, (myself included!), have trouble resisting them.

There are several ways to go about this. During barbecue season, you can toast the peppers on your outdoor grill over medium-hot coals, turning frequently, until all the skin is blackened and crisp. Indoors, you can get very similar results over a gas burner or under your broiler (grill). Or roast them in a very hot oven (500° F/250° C/gas mark 9), turning once, until the skin is completely charred.

Place the peppers in a plastic or paper bag for 10 minutes to allow them to sweat, then peel off the skin. Halve the peppers and discard the stems and seeds. Use immediately, or refrigerate or freeze for later use. They will keep for about 1 week in the fridge and 3 months in the freezer.

Clarified Butter

To prevent butter from burning during high-heat cooking, you can "clarify" it by removing its milk solids. Simply melt the butter over low heat, skimming off any foam. Then pour the liquid yellow fat carefully through a sieve, leaving any milky residue behind. This clarified butter will keep in the refrigerator for several months.

Ginger Juice

If you want zingy ginger flavor without chewing on stringy fibers, you can squeeze the juice from fresh ginger root with your garlic press. You'll need a piece of ginger approximately 1 inch by 2 inches to yield 1 tablespoon juice.

Herbs

The recipes in this book call for fresh herbs, not only for their lively, just-picked flavor, but because many of the delicate-leafed varieties, especially parsley, basil, cilantro and tarragon, lose a great deal of their character when dried. Some of the fuller flavored herbs, such as oregano, sage and rosemary, hold up much better under drying. However, because their flavor is more concentrated, use about one-third the quantity of fresh specified.

Toasted Nuts

Toasting nuts brings out their naturally rich, buttery flavor. Preheat the oven to 350° F/175° C/gas mark 4. Place nuts in a baking dish and toast them, shaking the dish occasionally, until the nuts are fragrant and golden brown anywhere from 7 to 15 minutes, depending on the nut. If toasting hazelnuts (filberts), rub them while still hot, a few at a time, in a clean dish towel to remove the skins. (Don't worry if all the skins don't come off.) Use immediately or freeze for up to 3 months. (Toasted nuts also make a great impromptu dessert topping!)

Olive Oils

These recipes use "pure" olive oil, unless otherwise specified, which tends to taste rather neutral and can withstand the high heat of sautéing or frying. The live oil terms "pure," "virgin" and "extra virgin" refer to the decreasing amounts of oleic acid in the oil and, usually, the increasing flavor complexity, quality and price. High heat, however, can destroy the finer oils, so use them to season freshly cooked pastas, brush them on just-grilled fish or feature them in a dressing laced with vinegar, citrus or wine.

Pepper

Unless otherwise specified, use black pepper, freshly ground, for the recipes in this book. For appearances' sake, white pepper is preferable in light-colored foods, such as cream sauces.

INDEX